Chameleon

Chameleon

The Lives of Dorothy Proctor

Dorothy Proctor
and
Fred Rosen

New Horizon Press   Far Hills, New Jersey

Requests for permission should be addressed to:
New Horizon Press
P.O. Box 669
Far Hills, NJ 07931

Dorothy Proctor and Fred Rosen.
    Chameleon
    The Lives of Dorothy Proctor

Library of Congress Catalog Card Number: 94-066762

ISBN: 0-88282-099-0
New Horizon Press

Manufactured in the U.S.A.

1998 1997 1996 1995 1994 / 5 4 3 2 1

Dedication

For my son Arthur. If I had to live my darkest hours over again to ensure you would be in my life, I would. Thank you for the light . . .

— D.P.

. . . and for the voices in the dark: Clint Walker, Will Hutchins and Ty Hardin.

— F.R.

Author's Note

This book is the autobiography of Dorothy Proctor. Everything is true, to the best of Ms. Proctor's recollection. Some of the conversations within the story have been reconstructed from interviews and research. The names of some individuals have been changed to protect their identities.

Table of Contents

Acknowledgements

The authors would like to thank the following:

James Dubro for opening some doors; Frank Weimann and Jessica Wainwright for putting us together; Rick Mofina of the Calgary Herald for his ethics and honor; Monica Zurowski, also of the Calgary Herald; Shara Spinks and the Fifth Estate for encouragement and support; Ann Petrie, likewise; Mr. and Mrs. McCree and their daughter "Kats" for their love; Robbie and Ron Wyenn who read an early draft and offered advice and shoulders to lean on; Ray Cardinal, who is always there; Calgary RCMP Narcotics Division, Calgary C.I.I.U. and Red Deer, RCMP, between 1980 and 1994; the Ontario Provincial Police between 1985 and 1994; and last but not least, all of the good guys out there who do their jobs in silent obscurity and make it easier for all of us to sleep at night.

Thank you all, and thank you to Joan Dunphy for making our vision a reality.

I hate because I am hated. I am hated because I let no one enter. Therefore they hate because they are rejected. Therefore I hate because they reject me. Who needs whom enough to try hard enough? To break down and annihilate what was once a strong fortress of transparent hate. I am dying in order to live.

— Dorothy Mills, Age 17

A nd if a man maim his neighbor, as he hath done, so shall it be done to him: breach for breach, eye for eye, tooth for tooth; as he hath maimed a man, so shall it be rendered unto him.

— Leviticus 24:19

Dorothy Proctor and Fred Rosen

CHAPTER ONE

Childhood

My first home, in Cape Britain, Nova Scotia, Canada, was a whorehouse. My mother ran it. My father Johnnie was a pond scum of a man, married to someone else. He lived with his wife. Our house was made of wood, with no basement. The outside was banked with peat moss to keep the cold air out and storm windows were left on all year 'round.

Bare floors inside the house, in all the rooms, no indoor plumbing and a narrow staircase leading to the upstairs bedroom. There was a coal stove near the backdoor, in the kitchen. The kitchen had a scarred, wooden table and iron folding chairs. I would sit there for hours, or minutes maybe. I'm not clear on measurements of time.

Anyway, I would press my face against the cold window pane and watch the wind whip up gales of wet snow, hoping the storm would get bad enough to keep the men away. If the men were caught in the house when the storm came up, as they often were, they just waited it out and got very drunk. When that happened, I would try and make myself very small, but it never worked.

People spent a lot of time indoors because the winters were long and cold. Summers were cool and short, with the threat of a storm always lurking off the Atlantic Ocean and the Gulf of St. Lawrence.

I remember always being cold.

1

The front room, as the parlor of our house was called—living room now—was always dark. In the daytime, people would walk by and figure the shades were pulled to keep out the sun. Not true. The shades were pulled to keep in the secrets.

Every once in awhile, three or four women would gather in the parlor and I would hear screams. After awhile, a woman would come out, sometimes my mother—blood all over her—and throw something in the stove. I was warm on days like that because the stove would be on full blast. I would be at the kitchen window watching the storm.

I remember bad smells, cries of pain and blood. Lots of blood.

Dorothy Proctor is the name I use, but it's not my real name, and I won't give out my birthdate.

You never give out your birth date. You never give out your real name. It's too easy to track someone down that way. I try to stay away from paper trails. That's a good idea when you have three contracts out on your life.

It's ironic, really. The contracts are for the good I've done in my life as an undercover agent, not the bad stuff I did when I was younger. There's a perverse sense of logic to it all, considering the background I come out of, a background that stretches back over a century into history.

I am a product of the Civil War. My paternal great, great grandfather was a slave who made it to Canada through the Underground Railroad. His son married a Mic Mac Indian. My great, great grandmother came to Nova Scotia with the Empire Loyalists and was connected to the English throne through the illegitimate line. Talk about dysfunctional. I'm related, albeit illegitimately, to the merry house of Windsor. She married a Black man. My great grandmother was then Black/White, French/English. My paternal grandparents were born in Nova Scotia, as was my father. My grandmother looked like a White woman so some of her kids were honey-skinned and some dark.

My father, Russell Ivan Mills, who everyone called Johnnie, was honey-skinned and considered handsome. This made him very popular with the ladies, who he treated very badly.

My maternal grandparents came from the Scottish Highlands and settled in Cape Britain. Some of my other relatives were Asians, Blacks, Caucasians and Indians. Some were very rich, others very poor, most were somewhere in between and many were criminals.

Cape Britain was made up mostly of Scots who had emigrated in the early 1800's. Fishing, farming and mining were the jobs of the day, but everything in Cape Britain smelled from fish. The men from the factory were always clumping by, their heavy shoes spattering mud puddles.

The town was also a seaport and troop depot. My mom, Mary Alice McDonald, took advantage of this itinerant population.

Mary Alice provided every service a thriving town needed. For the men, she owned and ran the local whore house. For the women, she acted as midwife and abortionist. And for everybody, she was a bootlegger who trafficked in rum. She was so rich that her rum boats were faster than the Coast Guard's, whose cutters they outran on almost a daily basis. But there were no hard feelings. She serviced those same Coast Guard sailors on their days off.

In between, Mary Alice always made time for the men in her life, especially my father. She had her cap set for Johnnie, but he was already married to someone else and much too young for her. She was almost twenty years older than Johnnie. Still, she made him feel like a king. He liked that, and began pimping for her.

At the time of my birth, none of Mary Alice's seven other children—by other men—lived in the home. They were all in orphanages. And even though there were reasons to believe that money was not an issue, the house was not in very good financial shape. I later found out that most of the money mother received, she spent on the men in her life. She dressed them and gave them cars and cash; there was not much left over for the house or me.

For me, the insanity began before the time most children have memories. But I can still remember. You never forget your first fearful vision.

The table of the high chair pushed against my chest. The strap across my bottom kept me in place. No matter how hard I struggled, I couldn't get out. I was a virtual prisoner. So I watched.

There on the bare linoleum floor, my father writhed on top of my mother, pushing harder and harder into her until finally, she gave a grunt and sagged back. The odor of sex filled the air.

I cried, just like always, out of need for love, for attention, for food, but mostly out of fear. My father looked up with this strange grin on his face and removed himself from my mother. There was this big thing sticking out from his body. He came over and bent down, passing his long, tapered fingers beneath my nose. The fingers reeked of sex.

"Shut your mouth, or I'll fill it," he threatened.

He did. Many times. I grew up thinking a penis was a teat.

Next memory. The brick chimney that ran through the upstairs bedroom. My crib was there, also a bed where I witnessed my mother and father on many occasions rutting like pigs, with no respect for the child watching.

During one of their love-making sessions, I started to cry. My mother picked me up and slammed me against the brick chimney.

Next memory. Watching my mother with other men, her customers. One of them was drunk and the man masturbated in front of me. Laughing, he climaxed on my head. As semen dripped down my face, my mother licked it off.

Next memory. My mother holding my vagina open, her customers rubbing their penis against me for excitement and later inserting themselves into my mother. No need to go on.

Any good memories?

None.

Going for a walk with mother and father?

Never.

Picking me up and swinging me around?

No.

Going on a picnic or to the beach?

No.

Hugs and kisses?

None.

But I do remember clean; even my mother's house was spotless. I always thought that was odd. Didn't clean mean good? Nevertheless, I developed a habit of cleanliness.

At six, I was old enough to tell people what was going on, but how? And who would believe me? I also stuttered so badly, I couldn't get anything out. People said that I was retarded. I heard them.

Johnnie, my father, didn't spend much time with my mother. He had other fish to fry and they always fought over that. One time, he disappeared for about four months. It was just assumed in the community that young Black men were off shacking up or seeking work. When their new sexual conquest faltered—and with it their erection—or the job ran out, they came home. No questions were asked. Johnnie was no exception. Whatever story he told was accepted. But for sure, he never told the truth.

After a while, Johnnie was finished with his wife, or she was finished with him, who knew? He turned to my mother, but only for a short period. Whatever the reason, it was time to move on, and he left. My mother took her anger out on me.

Once, Mary Alice got so mad at Johnnie, she took me by train to New Glasgow, Nova Scotia to his parents. She left me there. I didn't see Mary Alice again until I was fifteen years old. As for my father, he sent my grandparents $5.00 a week for my keep, no extras.

My grandmother was a severe looking women. She had strong, striking, almost manly features that only seemed feminine when she smiled—which she rarely did. I liked that though, when she smiled, because it lit up her face and she seemed like someone else.

My grandfather was short and well built, with high cheekbones; small ears that fell close to his head; a nose that fit his face and a small, almost feminine mouth.

My grandparents were very bourgeois—clean, well dressed, literate. They owned a trucking business and a salvaging company. They were not rich but much better off than most Blacks and many of the Whites. They had a nice home—shiny, waxed hardwood floors, good throw rugs, brass, lace, china and beautiful cut glass. Fine furniture. They were always well dressed, and had good cars. They were considered snobs by the community and they were not well liked.

Everything looked normal on the outside, but you never knew what was going to happen when the door closed at midnight.

Most of their twelve grown children were bad news. Rumors flew outside our house that they were whores, pimps, alcoholics, drug addicts, thieves, and child abusers. Violence was common, as was incest. Inside wasn't any better.

Great, huh? Out of one hell and into another. A new victim was *fresh meat*, and boy did they flock from all around to get their share. They sensed it was prey, like buzzards sighting on a wounded animal.

6

I soon labeled my grandfather as the son-of-a-bitch he was. He'd hunt me down until he had me alone in the garage or basement. Then he'd fondle me and later, make me sit on his lap with his penis sticking out of his pants. He'd push himself inside me, anus or vagina, whatever was comfortable for him.

I always walked around hurting, and I'd complain. My grandmother's response:

"You didn't wipe yourself good after using the bathroom. That's why you's so raw."

During this time, one of my uncles, Billy Sanford, came to live with us. Actually, Billy was my cousin, a product of a brother and sister incest union. He stalked me also. Mornings before going to school and later when the men came home from work, the game of avoidance began.

Weekends were the worst. Other men, uncles and cousins, would visit with their families and I was the main ticket. I would be made fun of in front of everyone, because I stuttered and seemed slow.

As for school, things were bad there too. I was starting to act out my problems. I couldn't learn and beat up my classmates. The teachers couldn't deal with me.

On top of all the confusion, an atmosphere of religious fanaticism engulfed me. A lot of the men who were abusing me and the women who looked the other way all attended church every Sunday. My grandfather was a deacon of our church and the whole family was very active there.

At home, my grandmother would force me to memorize scripture way beyond my level of understanding. Then I'd stand in Church every Sunday and recite—with my stuttering mouth— scripture after scripture, to the amusement of everyone.

No one outside the family would have known what was going on either. We looked like the perfect family in church. I sat between my grandparents, all dressed up with a silk ribbon in my hair, singing "Amazing Grace," in full voice. I heard people say that I was a pretty little child, but I had dead eyes.

What a way to meet God.

As for school, it was only a temporary respite. Besides, kids can be worse tormentors than their adult counterparts.

One day when I was about ten, I was walking home from school with four schoolmates, Tina, Julie, Cathy and Erica. The climate was hostile even though it was the start of the long, warm beautiful days of summer that only the Maritime Provinces are blessed with.

"Jesus Christ Dorothy, you have long Indian hair," said Julie.

"Your eyes are a little slanted, too" Tina added, stretching her own to mimic mine.

Cathy laughed. "Forget that. Hey, look at her ivory skin. Just what are you. Dorothy?"

"Black, white, chinko, domino!" they all yelled in unison.

"Nnno. . . nnno, ya ddon't unner. . . unner. . ."

"Domino, domino, domino, " they tormented me, all but Erica.

"See, my granppppppp. . . parents. . ." I looked at their faces and listened to their taunts. "Pa...pa...pick out friends....nnno...."

"What's the matter Dorothy, cccat, got your tttongue?" Julie mocked me.

Then, for some reason, I looked back at Erica. She had said nothing during all of this. Nothing. And she had a sneer across her face. That's when I knew with the second sense an abused kid develops about who's causing them harm: Erica'd put the others up to this. She'd manipulated them to make my life miserable. The hate swelled, and turned inside me; my stomach burned and I hit her hard. She hit me back but I not only was stronger, I hated more.

After it was over, Erica did not move for a long time. Her nose gushed blood and her glasses lay broken on the ground. Patches of her thick, mahogany brown hair were missing and she was crying. The others had backed off, scared to death of the violence I had unleashed from the core of my being.

Without stuttering, I said clearly, "You can all go straight to hell."

Later, my grandparents were outraged, not because I'd been fighting—after all, I was just following the family tradition—but because they had to pay to replace the glasses I'd broken.

"Dorothy, you acted like nothing better than common street trash," my grandmother said.

"Damn right," my grandfather agreed, "and I'll be damned if we'll have our family held up to public ridicule."

After that, I was driven to and picked up from school most of the time, which just led to more teasing.

I escaped into a fantasy world, where I would play act at being anyone, except me. I took to mimicking the people around me, but never, never a family member. There was not a person in my close family that I wanted to be. Instead, I imagined how I would become a teacher, the pastor's wife, a saleswoman and sometimes, neighbors.

Studying people became my avocation. I studied the way they acted, talked, walked and laughed, or better yet, what they laughed at. Hell, I didn't know what was funny. As for looks, that didn't matter. I knew if I could master their ways and commit them to memory, it would never be a problem wearing their skin. In my fantasy, I crossed color lines, religious boundaries and political beliefs.

Although I was living out a fantasy life in my head, I was also a stickler for reality, or what I perceived to be reality. The real people I knew in the community soon became boring and I realized I couldn't grow by doing the same mimicking of the same people all the time. I longed for the day I could mimic people who were really different from me. I found them at the movies.

It was then I began playing with my hair and some makeup to portray the different characters. I realized all the features on my face which kids made fun of could be assets—because of them, I could look Chinese or Indian or anything I wished to be.

And it was not only movies through which I learned my mixed up heritage could be a plus. When I met odd characters or learned real things in school, I filed the information in the "keep file" in my memory bank.

There were no good guys in my life. So my escape was in movies on Saturday afternoons. I loved watching cowboy two reelers. I'd sit in the dark at the movies and imagine that the hero would come and rescue me. I was so jealous of the heroine who had that wonderful man all to herself.

The cowboys were all tall and handsome, with crinkly smiles. I was certain that one day they were going to ride to my rescue.

No such luck.

But I had something in common with my reel heroes; I played a role in real life. I played the part of your average kid growing up in a normal family.

That was never who I was, of course. As I grew, the real me became a character in a film, with the insanity of my life a nonstop two-reeler in my head.

Other times, I relied on comics to take me away. Archie Comics activated one extreme fantasy. In it was Betty, my heroine—sweet, innocent and virginal.

But comics and movies were nothing but a brief respite. Most of the time, my family watched me like a hawk; I was a virtual prisoner in my own home. They kept me isolated from other people. I was like an animal being kept for his keeper's amusement.

Eventually, I discovered a technique to avoid being alone with the men in my family. It was the true start of my acting career.

I would become so ill that the doctor would be called. My acting was so good that I always convinced everyone, even the doctor, that something awful was wrong with me.

Over and over I would fall ill, but I would be well enough on Saturday to go to the movies and get some more ideas. This lasted so long that I was finally admitted to hospital for an appendix operation, during which it was discovered that I was damaged inside so badly from sexual abuse that corrective surgery had to be performed.

When the women in the family heard this, they branded me a whore because in their minds, I was a bad girl having sex with the boys. My family couldn't face the disgrace. They decided to ship me off to Boston, Massachusetts.

One thing that I couldn't understand was my family being embarrassed over something they thought I had done, in view of the fact that everyone in the family was an embarrassment, not only to the town but to me. The irony wasn't lost on me.

I got ready for my bus trip, a very long ride to the United States for a ten-year-old. It was not that I was afraid. I was a big girl for my age, and I never had a baby face. I was hard looking and never smiled. But I had never been allowed to be a child and now, I was packed off like a bag of unclean sheets to my relatives in Boston.

No way, though. No way was I going to give up and give in. Someplace, somehow, I'd make something of myself. Even if I had to go to hell and back.

As fate soon decided, hell's name was Boston.

CHAPTER TWO

Adolescence

I had met my aunt, Willena Shepard, and uncle, Benjamin Shepard, a few times when they came to Nova Scotia to visit. My aunt was my father's sister, and had moved to Boston as a young girl to avoid the scorn of the town.

She was in danger from the local women in New Glasgow because she bedded all their men. She hit pay dirt in Boston after a few months when she hooked up with a young, up-and-coming lawyer who set her up. She later married her pimp with the understanding that this lawyer would remain in her life. In return, the lawyer helped them get started in business. My aunt and uncle ended up owning the New England Real Estate Company and New England Oil.

Meanwhile, the world that I entered shook me up. This aunt and uncle were Black. They had bright respectability. My uncle was a Mason and my aunt was an Eastern Star, a member of black society. In fact she was so sought after that she was featured in the pages of *Ebony* magazine. They were members in good standing of the Episcopalian Church. Their business was doing well, and they had a live-in maid, owned two homes—one in fashionable Roxbury, the other a summer house on the Cape.

For a short while, things were better than they'd ever been. Then I learned they were also crazy. Once the novelty of having me with them dulled, they went back to their regular life. They partied all the time, drank heavily, had big fights and many sex partners. My uncle was very violent and beat me with a dog chain for any infraction.

After my uncle had completely terrorized me, he moved in for the kill and raped me. Soon, he was having intercourse with me at least three times a week. My aunt just let it happen. She was just interested in appearances, She made me call them "Mom" and "Dad." I lived in fear of "Dad" and had developed a couple more pathetic traits—bed wetting and wetting my pants.

Between ten and twelve, I witnessed a lot of criminal acts. I saw my first cousin, who I was calling brother by now, using drugs; I was always meeting his criminal friends. This introduced me to the drug trade early on in life, and taught me more than I realized at the time.

There were stolen goods in the house all the time. My aunt and uncle were friends with some heavy dudes. My uncle always carried a gun; so did my "brother."

The woman I called my "sister" was actually my half sister—Mary Alice's daughter. Mary convinced everyone that she was Johnnie's kid. She was not. The girl was Caucasian, but was forced to believe that she was half black. My aunt and uncle adopted her to improve their community image.

My half sister was always running away and being put into institutions and private schools. She also turned on me. Once, she stabbed me with a two-pronged fork in my leg and bit my arm so hard they had to pry her teeth from it. That was when I attempted to run away for the first time and failed. I began having daily nightmares.

School. God, it was just as awful there. I felt inadequate, without confidence. Every day I went to school, there was a fear in the pit of my stomach that someone would challenge me to a fight. It didn't make any difference why. And it always came to pass.

The first fight happened when one of my classmates, Ellen, taunted me.

"Gee Dorothy, you not too smart, are you?"

By this time, I'd become "incorrigible," or so some of the authorities decided.

On this fall afternoon, I'd concealed a stick in the small of my back. I pulled it out of the waistband, beat her again and again with it, to the cheers of my peers who had gathered after school to see me take her on. The cheers validated me, but after that, I was challenged at every turn by all the tough kids in my school who wanted to make their reputation. The stick soon gave way to chains, a rock in a sock, pepper that I could throw into an opponent's eyes, and then a special weapon that was used when I knew in advance there'd be a fight.

I found the razors in my uncle's medicine cabinet. He never even missed them. If there wasn't time to filch them, it was a simple matter to go into a drug store and buy them for a dime. That, and a little tape, and I was all set for the fight. And so they continued, as if on some schedule.

Always after school, always in the schoolyard, always a crowd around, and nearly always a bigger opponent than me. Usually girls, sometimes, guys. Didn't make any difference. I looked into their eyes and the hate came up, the hate that I had to keep submerged. The hate could finally and blessedly be let out on someone else.

Robyn was one of my opponents. She attacked one Thursday, coming in with a stick. I smiled and acted cool, just like a cowboy wading in with fists ready when it was ten against one, knowing in his heart that he represented right and he'd win no matter the odds. While occupied with my daydream, my hand would come up in a slap . . . and the fight would be over.

The noisy crowd suddenly went dead. Robyn just stood there, stunned, feeling something wet on her face, slowly going into shock. And then she put a disbelieving hand up to her face and it came away dripping blood from the long gashes on her cheeks.

I tossed my head. The razor blades were taped between my fingers, where no one could see them at first glance, and when I slapped a person back and forth, they would be laid open. The fight was always over quickly.

If you're ever looking to recruit someone tough to help you with a job, don't hire the person who has the scars. Hire the one who gave the person the scars.

As for my aunt and uncle, they knew nothing about any of this. The code of the streets dictated silence.

I started to test, running away at twelve. Not in the traditional sense, though.

I started by not going home after school. During my time away, I'd meet other kids like myself. We stayed around the schoolyard or went for bus rides all over Boston. As a result, when I showed up after supper, I knew they would beat me; I knew I would be grounded, but grounded from *what* I never knew, as I had no privileges anyway.

After awhile, the big kids would let us hang out with them. They had cars and smoked; sometimes they had beer. I started to stay out longer, so long in fact that the police would come looking for me.

I now had older girl friends who would let me stay over night. Their parents never asked any questions; so it was easy. My new friends would recycle me between them. I managed to stay away for weeks at a time.

The girls were much older, maybe seventeen or eighteen, and would take me to their hangouts. Boston is a seaport, just like Cape Britain— lots of young sailors. The big girls dressed me up, put makeup on my sullen face, and I looked at least sixteen.

It worked. I was sullen so the sailors were impressed and mistook sullen for sexy. I became very popular with my new found friends. They saw me as fearless, because I was always doing something crazy to impress them. I became more daring as time passed.

I got to know a lot of young sailors. They were far from home and would hang out with us. The sailors would take us on their ships. Very rarely was sex involved. We were just some group of young people seeking comfort in each others' company. But when there was sex with a sailor, they always offered a gift. Not money, but some little thing to show some appreciation, an act of kindness that I was not used to.

One sailor, Mac Jason, brought me shoes when he came to port. He saw that I always had holes in my shoes and walked funny, because they were too small. Mac felt sorry for me and was kind. Still, I could never take anything back to the house. I left my new things at my friends' houses.

To this day, I can't understand why a rich Boston family like mine, with a big house in the city, a country home, maid, new cars, furs, lots of jewelry, wouldn't buy me shoes when I needed them. I was always ashamed going to school, and it was hard for me to walk. If I tried to borrow my "sister's" shoes, I would get beat up.

Eventually, the abuse my family inflicted on me no longer worked. My aunt and uncle lost all control of me.

The longer I stayed away, the more I learned. That meant power and I was gaining it fast. Meanwhile, my Boston family had had enough of me. I was now a public embarrassment; the kid that was always running away and being returned by the cops. That did nothing for my "Father's" and "Mother's" social standing.

I became conscious of a murderous spirit growing in me at about the same time I was sent back to Canada for the last time. The plan was for me to take a plane to Toronto. Johnnie, my father, would meet me at the airport and put me on a train back to my grandparents in Nova Scotia.

On the plane, my fantasies occupied my entire trip, how someday I was going to kill them, all of them, hands on, one murder at a time. Just wait until I grew bigger and had some money, they all would pay big time.

By this time, I thought that I could live on my own. I was willing to work. I would lie about my age, but how to get away and what to do? Anything and anywhere would be better than going back to Nova Scotia.

When the plane landed in Toronto, my father was there with his latest woman friend, Gail, to pick me up.

"You're a whore, Dorothy, nothing but a whore," he said to me, as Gail stood there listening. I looked away, terribly embarrassed, yet the anger rising in me. "And don't ever use my last name," he added for good measure.

This last request was no problem for he used different last names - McDonald, Mills, Shepard, Prevoe, so names didn't matter to me. Not being related to him was okay with me. Johnnie had a hell of a lot more to be ashamed of than I did.

Anyway, I stayed over night with Gail, who lived with her girlfriend in a small apartment. I later found out that Gail was a whore and Johnnie was her pimp.

The next day, before he put me on a train to Halifax, where my aunt and uncle were supposed to drive from New Glasgow to get me, Johnnie sat me down.

"I've got something to tell you," Johnnie said.

I don't know why he picked that time and that place, but he told me about the time after I was born, when he'd left and befriended the Chinese man in Halifax, and his subsequent adventure in Communist China.

"Let's just say that I performed a valuable service for one of our distant Chinese relatives, in cooperation with certain corrupt Canadian officials," he said. "It is a service so important that you will benefit from it for the rest of your life." He stopped to stare at me for a moment. "If you so choose.

18

"And what is the favor?" I asked.

"Mah May Wan," Johnnie said, ignoring me.

"Huh?"

"That is your Chinese name."

"You're kidding."

"No, I'm dead serious. Your Chinese name is Mah May Wan. Because you are under the protection of the ancient Mah Clan, you will be accepted into any of the Chinatowns of the world. Wherever you go, you will have a safe haven. You will also be given the names of some high ranking Triad members, the Chinese Mafia, to use so that you can gain entry into Chinese society."

A lot of good that did me then. In the meantime, my father was abandoning me again.

So fuck Johnnie with his favors.

My aunt and uncle, they were two winners. Everyone in three towns and two cities knew what kind of man my uncle was. He had children all over the place and he abused many of the females in his and his wife's families. He ran around with friends of his wife's. She claimed to never see a thing.

I made up my mind. These were not people with whom I was going to go home. With one large suitcase and ten dollars, some street smarts and a lot of nerve, I got off at the last stop before Halifax. My destination was Halifax all right, but not to my aunt and uncle's house.

I began hitchhiking. I gave each driver a made-up story. It was fun. I could be anyone I wanted to be, and I didn't have to spend a lot of time with any one person. Still, there were things I had to learn about hitchhiking.

Never get into a car or truck with more than one man.

Stick to older men who are easier to manipulate.

Make sure no one is hiding in the back seat.

If the driver is drinking, never get in.

New cars mean a meal or maybe some money.

All of these things were learned by trial and error the first time out.

When I arrived in Halifax, I was $50 ahead of the game. I checked into the YWCA. They didn't ask for identification. I paid for a few days up front, had a bath and slept the sleep of the dead. I had every intention of looking for a job the next day.

The following morning, I talked myself into a job as a waitress in a hash joint near the waterfront. I had stopped stuttering when I ran away from home the first time. It would start again only when I was with my family. So I could talk plain enough. But I was so poor in math, it was hard for me to add up the bills.

My boss Henry Hennessee was a nice man, but he had to think of his restaurant. He put me in the kitchen to wash dishes.

A week later, a cop came up behind me.

"Dorothy Shepard?"

Turning I wiped the soapsuds from my hands and swallowed. "Yes?" This guy had nothing better to do than track down a twelve-year-old, I guess. Well, he had succeeded. Damn him.

My aunt and uncle came for me and took me back to New Glasgow. Trapped again.

I was returned to my grandmother, who found me a job at an old folks home for $15 a week. Ginger Peters, who owned the home, worked me hard. Every day I was on my knees, scrubbing hard wood floors with a scrub brush and a bar of lye soap.

There was a small store in front of the home owned by Mrs. Peters's son. I had to wait in front of the store every day for a bus to go home. Like clockwork, Frank Peters came out to wait with me. He wasn't there to keep me company, though. He showed me dirty pictures. He sold pornography on the side.

One day, he asked me to help him carry some stuff from the room in the back of the store to the front. "I'll pay you five dollars," he said. When I got to the back, Frank slammed the door shut and said, "Suck me." I got sick all over his shoes, not only because of the act but because of the smell—he was so very dirty.

He got real mad at me and kicked me out. "If you ever tell anyone what happened, I'll hurt you bad." I went home knowing that I had to get away.

The next day was Saturday and I volunteered to go to the store for my family. Walking over to the cash register, I opened it, took the money and ran.

Outside the store, I put out my thumb to hitchhike and got a ride fast. A man going to Trurio—the next town.

I knew I could not hide out there for more than a day or two, because we knew a lot of people there and most of them were related to us. I decided to head for Montreal.

In my mind, I went over everything I'd heard about Montreal. I knew I had family there.

I hitched with truck drivers, who weren't so bad. They fed me and gave me some money. I only had to sleep with a few as payment for the ride, but I got more out of them by way of information: what companies to ride with, where to stay when I got to Montreal, and where to look for work if I was underage. The clubs and bars that were owned and operated by the Mob hired and paid under the table.

Some of the truckers were connected and dropped many "wiseguy" names. It is not true that bad guys don't talk. The only ones that don't talk much about what they do and who they know are the "shooters," and given the right circumstances, they also talk.

One thing the truckers did not tell me was how to stay cool with the cops. As I was not yet connected, I got hassled a lot. However, I managed to stay away from them, at least for a while.

Learning, learning, always learning.

I found the right neighborhood. It was wild. Music, dancing, freedom, style. Big cars, beautiful people, exciting night spots. I found work cleaning bathrooms, washing dishes, running errands at night. I would sometimes fill in for the bus person and wait on tables when the clubs got real busy. I would do anything to live and work where the action was.

Some of the hookers I met thought that I was pretty and just needed some clothes and a hair dresser. My body was good, well developed for my age, but I always covered it up with loose fitting clothing. Strangely, I was shy and bold at the same time. I don't know how the two worked together, but for me they did, so I cultivated this persona to the max.

I was constantly shocking people by word or deed. This underage, drab, underweight bush baby. For example, I would raise hell with pimps. I hated them. When they started sniffing around me, I would curse them and threaten to hit them. The hookers would have a fit and would worry about me and the gangsters would laugh because they hated pimps too.

Gangsters were the bosses in Montreal; pimps had to lay low. Most of the pimps came from the United States. Pimping was a lifestyle they were used to, but they could not push the girls around like in the United States. Also, they couldn't run a "stable."

I can't remember any pimp having more than one girl at a time in Montreal back then, unless he brought his stable from the States with him. The entrepreneurial spirit in us would laugh at those girls and secretly admire the pimp.

Most of the Canadian girls only tricked as a side line to another job. They were not career hookers. They could be selective and had more control of their lives. And the Canadian men, somehow they knew that being a pimp was not a job for a real man. So they all had jobs too—bouncers, bartenders waiters, taxi drivers, something that would keep them close to the action. Most of them gambled on cards and horses and had a partnership with their girlfriends, sometimes even married them.

The rooming house I lived in was two blocks from the "strip," where all the clubs were. The entertainers who had not made it big, mostly band members, chose to stay in my rooming house when they played town. The older ones came mostly from the South, untrained, poor but risk takers. I *liked* risk takers. I was never a groupie, exactly, but I enjoyed listening to the bands talk into the wee small hours of the morning around a big old kitchen table. They talked about playing back-up for some big performer. They had traveled the world, seen it all and they were full of life and pride, never giving up, always reaching. The older ones looked after the young musicians, mostly from New York, Detroit and Chicago, and gave them the benefit of their years of experience, becoming their mentors.

Every once in a while, their spark would ignite something deep down inside me, pride in who and what I was. But just as quickly, something inside or outside would extinguish it.

CHAPTER THREE

The Underworld

I began to steal, nothing big, just small things. Sometimes I'd get caught. Since I never had enough money to pay the cops off, which would have resulted in dropped charges, I was instead shuttled off to jail.

During one of my visits to Fulum Jail, I met a girl who was much older than I was, almost twenty. I had seen her before in the holding cells downtown. Everyone knew her as a tough girl by reputation. Her name was Kitty.

Kitty came from Point St. Charles, a poor Irish neighborhood in Montreal. She had beautiful titian colored hair and creamy white alabaster skin, belied by a face that had a perpetual scowl. Because of the scowl and a broken and flattened nose, she looked like a hard drinking, Irish tough.

Kitty had a foul mouth that she often backed up with her fists. No experienced girl was crazy enough to take her on. The young ones just stayed away from her. In spite of the uglier aspects of her personality, she seemed to be respected by the guards; she even played cards with them. Unlike the way she treated the girls, she smiled, small-talked and kidded the guards. As I watched, I learned. It seemed to me that Kitty and the older girls knew how to play the game. They were treated better.

Because of my toughness and bravado, the older girls started to notice me. Kitty took a liking to me, took me under her wing and became my mentor.

"Dorothy, you have to learn to chill out when you're inside," she would drill into my head. "The idea is to *charm* them."

That was a revolutionary concept. By copying the older girls, especially Kitty, I learned to charm the guards, and got more privileges, like extra food, candy and smokes.

Soon, I was learning how to manage my anger, so I wouldn't be hurt by it. Under Kitty's patient guidance, I became sweet as molasses, at least with the guards: flashing smiles, batting eyelashes, giggly and oh-so-submissive; all the while a dangerous undercurrent of rage boiled away on the back burner.

Kitty taught me how to wear make-up, dress, walk; things that would help me get results on the street and would make me acceptable to the more classy group of street people. While we served together inside, I was never in trouble. Not once.

Over time, I realized that Kitty had a soft side she did everything to hide, especially when it came to the Catholic religion. Nuns and priests were demigods to her, earthly deities whose edicts could not be questioned by the less than chosen. Yet, when it came to having premarital sex, she went against the core of her religion.

The one thing she never stopped talking about was her boyfriend. It was her boyfriend this and her boyfriend that. She would sit for hours entertaining us with stories about their sex lives together, laughing in her high bawdy house laugh at their adventures in love together. But Kitty also had her secretive side: she would never reveal his name. She was afraid one of us would look him up and steal him.

Eventually, our sentences were getting worn down and we were close to release. Kitty was going to be released onto the street two weeks before me. Because I was younger, the terms of my release were different. I would have to stay in a half way house for awhile and go back to school. This had happened before, and usually I ran away as soon as I could.

"Dorothy, listen, if you do run away again, look for me at Club Beaucoup," Kitty told me. That's where she hung out. She gave me the address of the club. "I'll have lookouts," she continued, "in case I'm not there. They'll take you to me."

That's exactly what happened. I ran from the halfway house within twenty four hours of my release. Club Beaucoup was easy enough to find but no Kitty.

"I'm looking for Kitty," I told Amy, one of the girls who was hanging out at the bar. "We were in detention together. My name's Dorothy."

Oh, yeah, Kitty said you might be showin' up." Amy wrote down an address and handed it to me.

I went to the address she gave me and found Kitty's pad, an apartment above a store. The vestibule that led inside was narrow, just enough room for one person to pass. Then there was a flight of dirty stairs that creaked on the way up. The air smelled from something foul, like cabbage and rotten eggs mixed together.

Light bulbs were missing. Deep shadows gave way to glaring light. The paint was peeling. Kitty had been so clean and tidy in jail. What the heck was she doing living in a dump like this?

My knock on the door was quickly answered by a very tall, muscular, man. To me, he looked about twenty-five, at least.

"Kitty's not here," he told me in answer to my question.

"Well, we met in detention and she said I should look her up after I got out."

He smiled. He had nice teeth. "Fine, why don't you come on in and wait."

I found myself in a shabby sitting room furnished with Salvation Army furniture. A small kitchen was off to the left. A scarred door, half hanging on one hinge, led to the bathroom.

"I'm Bobby," the tall, blond man said by way of introduction. And that's all he said. He never revealed his status to me and I never asked.

Bobby took out some Labatt's Fifty. After four or five bottles, we were in bed and going at it. No big deal. Or maybe it was in a sense. A lay for five beers. At the time, it seemed a fair trade to me.

Kitty still hadn't shown up, so after awhile, I washed up. Before I left, Bobby pressed something into my hand. On the way downstairs I didn't notice the dirt and I didn't smell the stink. There, nestled in my palm, was a brand new twenty dollar bill. Not bad. Not bad at all. I walked on air all the way back to the club.

Kitty got there about an hour later. She wore a bold flower printed polyester dress which swished around her short legs as she moved toward me in her stiff-legged stride. I saw storm clouds rising. When she got in striking distance, her fist flashed forward, too quick for me to block it, and I was hit with a punch that was hard enough to make my teeth rattle.

The punch stunned me; she was so fast, I couldn't fight back. All I could do was cower into a self protective ball as she rained blows down upon me. The bouncer finally stepped in and separated us.

"What the hell is wrong with you?" I shouted.

"What the hell is wrong with me? With me?" Kitty screamed.

She lunged toward me and the bouncer held her in check.

"Who the hell do you think you slept with this afternoon, you little tramp?"

I thought for a second. Oh shit.

"He's your boyfriend?"

Kitty nodded.

It was common, in girl's apartments, to find men who were only friends or hiding out from the law. You just never asked why they were there. Why was she mad at *me*? Bobby knew the score and he never let on. Maybe she couldn't take it out on him and I was elected.

"And you took money from him, you little whore."

Great. That made matters worse. In her eyes, that made her man a trick.

I don't know why Bobby told her, maybe to hurt her, who knows. But down there on the ground, as I was planning my paybacks, one idea flashing in my mind was to take Bobby away from her and dump him. That would pay them both back good.

Later that night, I sat in Hal's, a squalid little diner in the red light district, with all the whores. I was drinking a cup of coffee, smoking a cigarette and plotting my revenge. My next move would be an act of violence to be sure. For no reason in particular, I glanced out the window and saw a woman passing. She had two black eyes, her face was unrecognizable and her jaws were wired shut. "Bad date," I mumbled.

The woman stopped for a moment, turned and looked in the window. She saw me; we made eye contact and tears squeezed out of her puffed up, black and blue eyes.

My God! It was Kitty.

She was still standing there when I ran to get her and pulled her inside to my booth. There I was one moment plotting my revenge and the next helping her. Go figure.

With her jaws wired shut, she couldn't talk, so she wrote everything down.

"I got drunk after I hit you," and she smiled weakly, the old, friendly Kitty again, "and went after Bobby. This is what he did to me," pointing at her face and crying.

It was me. Me. I was the cause. People were always getting hurt over me. Damn.

I stared at her. Kitty was a wreck, just the way I'd wanted her not more than a few minutes before she showed up. I'd gotten my revenge without having to lift a finger. But I didn't feel very good about it. Did I have a heart after all?

I looked after Kitty for two months. She lived with me in my room. I paid for her medicine, let her wear my clothes and bought her toiletries and also paid for her special diet. All the while I was getting a reputation on the street as a solid broad.

When she was on her way to recovery, Kitty started to go out more and more. She would leave in the morning, hair combed and make-up neat. When I saw her in the evening, she looked disheveled and smelled from booze. She was back to turning tricks and turning low level scams. It was time to move on.

We never talked about separation. Street people never got too deep with one another. Things were clear to us and we didn't worry about appearances like straight people did. When we made up, it was real until the next time we fought. We knew that for most of us there wouldn't be a "years later." We took care of things as they happened. Something very serious had to happen to carry a grudge.

A short while later, Kitty and I said our goodbyes. Kitty went back to what she knew—Bobby. No recriminations. It was our way, our thing, the way of the street.

I hitched a ride to Vancouver, reconnecting with the West Coast action. I befriended a hooker in Vancouver, who had a black boyfriend who was a soldier. He would come up from Seattle every week to spend time with her. We partied together for awhile.

When I finally returned to Montreal, I never tried to find Kitty and Bobby. By that time, in my own mind, I had risen higher than that. There was no room in my life any more for the likes of them. They just didn't have what it took to rise above their lot in life.

Kitty would always be satisfied turning ten dollar tricks and getting drunk every night in sleazy bars. And Bobby? The biggest job he would ever do was to pull a stick-up whenever it seemed cool and the pickings good. Their biggest dream would be to *buy* a car instead of stealing one.

That mind set wasn't for me. I was better than that. A lot better. I was a class act, or at least, I was going to be one I thought with the incredible aspirations of the young.

When I appeared on the streets after my absence from taking care of Kitty, everyone was happy to see me. I got right back into the thick of things, pulling scams. I embarked on a series of jewelry heists.

I was approached by professional thieves. Because I was very agile, they wanted me to climb through windows or small openings and let them in to the stores we would rob. Then I would act as a lookout. Once the job was finished, I would help them carry the goods out.

Within an hour after the score, the goods would be turned over to a backstreet fence, who would give us a third on the dollar for the jewelry. Then I would take my money, go out and celebrate and go on about my business.

I did a couple of those jobs. Each time I returned from a score, I entertained my friends with stories of my adventures. I would made sure that my stories were peppered with anger towards the police and judges. I made them sound like the stories I heard from the people fresh out of the joint. Soon, I earned the nickname "Little Gangster."

I ran wild through the streets of Montreal, sometimes teaming up with other young renegades on scams, but soon, going off again on my own.

I enjoyed being a loner. I didn't like routine and I hated to depend on anyone or have them depend on me. I couldn't live by the clock, since I had none; so I would miss appointments or forgot what day I was supposed to do something. Then I would get the travel bug and end up, as Willie Nelson would say, on the road again.

Before I was fifteen I had hitched across Canada at least four times. I had also hitched rides from Montreal to Boston, New York, Detroit and Chicago. As I did more and more jobs, I made friends in all of these places. Still, I had not yet broken through to the top ranks of criminals, but I was on my way.

In Montreal, as in other big towns, stars performed at clubs all year round. I saw many of the shows. I hung out in bars day and night, in every city, town or hamlet I visited. It didn't matter who was billed—I'd be there.

There were no concerts in those days, because the clubs were large enough to accommodate the big bands and floor shows. Aaron Neville, Harry Belafonte, Patti LaBelle, The Sweet Inspirations with Sissy Houston, Frank Sinatra, Jr. and his dad, the legendary Muddy Waters, Smokey Robinson and the Miracles, Little Stevie Wonder, Etta James, Billy Daniels, and many, many more. These big acts loved performing in Montreal and when I was there, I saw them. I got to know many of the performers on a personal level, from the band members to the headliners.

I slept with a lot of them, as did most young women on the scene; broke bread with most, got drunk and did drugs with some. From these encounters, I gleaned as much information as my brain could store. I learned where they came from, what it was like, who the players were and where the main hangouts in each city were located.

When I went there, I would know that there was a hotel called the Mark Twain at 111 Division Street in Chicago, and that a doorman by the name of Roger would, for a price, help a girl get a date with a Sugar Daddy.

Before I got to New York, I knew most of the bartenders' names at the popular watering holes. Hell, I knew that there was a bar called The Stage Door next door to the Apollo Theatre, where the bands hung out.

New York, Chicago, Philadelphia, Boston, Detroit and so many other cities— I listened and learned.

Boston I knew as a small child, and I had spent many hours in Detroit but I didn't know the nightlife. Because of my Montreal contacts, when I later visited these places I could actually walk in to a local bar, call the bartender by name and go directly to the bathrooms or pay phones because I knew exactly where they were.

I practiced my image and ethnic persona for each city until it was so correct, I was never looked upon as a stranger in the neighborhood I wanted to get into. I knew stories that only a regular customer would know and I was bold enough to get into intimate conversations about past events. I was so good that when a customer would be a bit suspicious of me, someone would always vouch for me.

This was my life at the time, my schooling, and I was good at it. I learned to check out *everything*. No matter what information I got, I double checked it with my street contacts.

As for the stars in the bars, after awhile, I'd hung out with them so much that I was no longer impressed by them. I learned from intimate experience that they put their pants on one leg at a time just like everyone else and, contrary to what television and the movies would have you believe, stars actually went to the bathroom just like regular folk.

As time went on, I became more used to them and stopped standing in line to see them perform, and wasn't flattered if they payed any attention to me. I did, however, appreciate their God-given talent and hard work. I was a fan of many, but I didn't see them as the demigods the media set them up to be or better than me. After all, like I said, I've see many with their pants down.

No big thing.

My heroes are not celebrities, big shots or the very rich. My heroes are farmers, especially farmers' wives, charwomen, single parents who make an effort to raise their children with dignity, kindergarten teachers, street cleaners—men and women who are not afraid of dirt or hard work and can still smile and exchange a joke at the end of the day.

I come from a diverse heritage, but put them all together and they are a people who like to fish, fuck, fight and get tight—people who can slip a lie in a conversation so skillfully that it won't hit you until you're in bed at 2 a.m. A slippery group, every last one of us.

I learned very early on that if you were a freeloader, you would not be welcomed in *any* inner circle. Money was very important. As a free agent, I'd learned to hold my own. That meant I bought my own drinks, payed for a round, shared taxi fares, and covered charges in the clubs. All this put me in a position to be invited to in-house parties where I would be chosen from time to time to be the star's date for the evening.

Most of them were very kind and generous, and I tried as best I could to stay away from the freaks— they were always on the hunt for a target, a victim, and runaways like me were ple ntiful and available.

One party I went to in Montreal involved Thomas Morgan, the singer. He was best known for his theme song and he projected a cool, controlled persona on stage with his smooth growl of a voice. He was always immaculately dressed in a tuxedo and with his hair carefully coiffed. That night long ago he walked over and sang to our table.

There were three very beautiful young women at that table. I was a dishrag in comparison. High fashion was definitely not my strong suit, but I was always clean and honest in my unadorned style. Given all of that, I found myself favored with good fortune.

A short while after Thomas went back to the stage, the maitre d'hotel came over. "Chickie, I have something here for you," he said. I knew he was nothing more than a *maquereau* (pimp), which became obvious after he passed me a folded, white piece of stationery

"I would like the pleasure of your company after the show. I'm staying in the Queen Elizabeth Hotel, Room 222.—Thomas Morgan"

When I arrived at the hotel, Mr. Morgan's bodyguard was waiting in the lobby for his master's guest. He passed me upstairs to Thomas's room very quickly.

It wasn't a room actually, but a salon or suite. I had seen better. Lots of guests were packed inside. I wasn't impressed by the place or by Thomas Morgan; I mean, no one was tearing off their clothes to be with him. Not me or any of the others who were hanging out.

"What'd ya think of my performance tonight? I was great, wasn't I?"

I didn't answer immediately.

"Wasn't I?" Thomas repeated, not without a little bombast.

"Sure," I said enthusiastically.

I wasn't about to blow a safe, warm, nice, big clean bed—not to mention name instead of bar brand drinks, rich food and maybe a good connection—because of his Empire State Building-sized ego.

It took an hour or so for his guests to fawn all over themselves in their compliments to the great man and score their points, until finally, with a closing of the door, the last one left.

"And now you, Chickie," Thomas said, smiling and advancing toward me.

After a feeble attempt at foreplay, we stripped and got into bed. I gently pushed his head down between my legs. (They say they don't do it; they *all* do it.)

I was enjoying myself, thinking about a good night's sleep on a soft bed. As I reached over and clutched the side of his head in fake passion, my ring got caught in his hair. Pulling it, I saw something in my hand.

"Aagh!" I screamed, looking at a hairy thing that resembled a mink pelt in my hand. It was his toupee.

Scalping was a first for me; my family had told me early on that scalping had been started by white men, a practice Indians had picked up on. However, to the best of my knowledge, I was the only modern-day woman of Mic Mac Indian heritage who had ever been responsible for scalping an entertainer.

After the initial shock wore off, I did what any sane person would do. I laughed and laughed, holding up my furry prize in awe.

"I think you'd better leave now," Thomas informed me gravely, trying as hard as he could to hold on to whatever dignity he had left.

"You're no lady," he added solemnly, and pressed twenty dollars in my hand for taxi fare.

"And you're worth just about this much," I said, holding the bill up in my fist.

I can still see the bewildered and hurt look on his face. Betrayed by a fourteen-year-old. He was lucky a cop didn't bust him for doing it with a minor.

I liked living in Montreal. Everyone knew what was expected of them and they could get as big as they wanted to within their own backyards. When that happened, they would be at a level to have an audience with the shadow people, "The Mob."

Everyone knew who the Mob was. It was the Mafia.

When I finally met the Godfather, it was by accident. I was raising a ruckus outside the Rodeo Bar.

"Hey, get outta here!" yelled the manager.

"Blow me," I yelled back, grabbing my crotch and laughing.

The small crowd that had gathered laughed along with me, but when the white Cadillac Sedan De Ville, about a block long, pulled up to the curb, everyone became silent. A beefy looking guy behind the wheel, opened the door, got out, walked to the rear door and with a half bow, opened it.

Out stepped a man of medium height, with a hard, swarthy face, his hair slicked back into a pompadour and parted neatly to the side. He was immaculately dressed in a black gabardine suit, button-down black shirt and bright red tie, a red handkerchief peeking from his breast pocket.

"What the hell's going on here?" the man growled to the manager at the door.

The manager, beads of perspiration popping out on his forehead, came running over.

"Oh, Mr. Cotroni, I'm so sorry, I . . ."

My eyes widened and I stopped, listening to the conversation. The elegant man was Frank Cotroni, one of the most powerful members of the Montreal mob. He owned all of the city's rackets—drugs, gambling, protection, cops on the pad—you name it and the Cotronis, that is Frank and his younger brothers Vince and Pepe, controlled it all.

"Huh, huh, so this kid is making noise and keeping people out of my bar," Frank rumbled at his man, then turned to me. "Well, what kind of work do ya do, kid?"

"Whatever I feel like," I said defensively. "It's a free country, and I got a right to be wherever I want to be."

Frank smiled. "You know who I am?"

I shook my head no. "You're a big guy in a fancy suit in a big car." I was lying of course, and he knew it. Everyone knew who Frank Cotroni was.

Frank laughed. "You got nerve kid, that I'll say for ya. What's ya name?"

"Chickie," I said, using my street name of the moment.

"Well, what kind of work do ya do, Chickie?"

"This and that. Nothing I want to discuss in public. Buy me dinner and I'll tell you more."

Frank laughed again, a big hearty chuckle. "Well kid, I think you're a little too young for me. You might give me a heart attack. Tell you what."

He reached in his coat, came out with a card and handed it over. "If you ever want to do some real work, give that guy on there a call and tell him it was at my recommendation."

I glanced at the card. There was a name and number and that was all.

"See ya," he said as he went past, and lightly patted my head, "and stop making noise in front of my bar."

His look told me he was serious.

Almost a week went by before I decided to call the number.

"Oh yeah, Mr. Cotroni said you might call," said the voice on the other end of the line. His name was Chuck Higgins.

We made a date to meet. Chuck and I hit it off and he became my mentor. He taught me how to be a runner for the mob. I would run anything—numbers, drugs, counterfeit money, whatever it took. No job was too dangerous for me. After awhile, the rest of the boys thought I was downright crazy. I'd go places and take risks that none of them twice my age would dare to do.

As I made my way around, one thing I would hear over and over from the wiseguys: stories about New York City. When some of them returned after three or four months, even a year away, everyone would gather around and listen to their war stories. To hear them tell it, New York was lawless. One could do anything one had the balls for. Money was the key to success and if you had enough, you were safe. Nothing could touch you. But we were warned. You had to have guts to live in New York.

As I saw it, New York was the gangsters' finishing school. I dreamed of going there and hitting it big.

Meanwhile, my work with the Cotronis brought me into a very different group of people than I had ever known. I entered "Cafe Society." I made money through the week, running errands for the Cotronis, passing bad checks and counterfeit money. I was also handling two sugar daddies and I was crazy trying to juggle them. They always wanted a date on Friday or Saturday night, and I wanted those nights for myself.

I liked the glamour of Friday and Saturdays and I loved how I was being accepted by the middle- and upper-class people who bought any story I had a mind to tell them.

My stories and looks varied with my mood. I was a Eurasian dancer, a French model, a Black show girl. I was a rich English playgirl, the daughter of a captain of industry, everyone except what I really was—a slick, mongrel street kid trying to put one over. Being the toast of some popular night clubs where the professional working-class and high-class *bon vivants* hung out, I met up with a real model from Martinique, Barbara, a beautiful, blond-haired, elegant woman who was dating a very successful Montreal doctor.

I had admired this couple from afar for weeks and dreamt of being part of their crowd. At last, there they were talking to *me*. They asked me to join them and we danced, drank and laughed the night away.

As the night moved toward the next day, we gathered more of their friends, and we all ended up at Barbara's apartment. Somehow, I'd ended up with Pierre, a handsome pilot from Paris. He flew between Paris and Montreal and was leaving for home the next night and he wanted me. Well, I wanted him.

Drinks were served as we settled in for a visit— a short one, I hoped. I wanted to get Pierre to a hotel fast.

Then the atmosphere changed.

First the drugs came out: coke and weed. I was shocked. These people doing drugs! I thought only low lifes did drugs, not rich, well educated people of breeding.

Well, I was not going to do drugs with them, so I passed. After about an hour, couples started to openly fondle each other, removing their clothes. Although I'd had plenty of private experience by now, I was very shy about sex in public. It was another matter behind closed doors with my partner.

Before I knew it, Pierre was all over me. All hands and mouth. When I tried to convince him to leave with me for the hotel, he drew back insulted. "I want to be part of the scene," he insisted. "You'll love it."

"I'm not taking part in any, any . . ." and I looked around me at the writhing bodies, "orgy," I finished.

Pierre got mad, got up, walked over to Barbara who was surveying the sea of bodies admiringly. "She won't join in," he said angrily. Barbara beckoned me over with a red-tipped manicured finger.

The floor was full of arms and legs, men and women, men and men, women and women. Naked flesh slapped together. It was a frenzy of debauchery, unlike anything I knew. I walked carefully. I didn't want to step on people.

"What do you mean you won't take part, Chickie?" said Barbara, pouting. "You should be grateful to be part of the inner circle. How dare you refuse to take part? After all," and her lean arm swept across the room in a grand gesture, "all my guests are very important people—doctors, judges, lawyers. Get with it. Grow up or get out!"

I left, crying. I had thought I was rising above my background and moving with better people. I had looked up to these people. How dare they lie to me with their sophisticated and respectable facade? They were pigs! I knew plenty of that kind already.

It was my first lesson in mistaken identity. Everything is not always what it seems to be.

I went back to hanging out as usual with a rag-tag bunch, when I fell in with a group of Trinidadians. They were free spirits. Singing and dancing was a way of life for them. I seemed to fit in well and started to date Louis, a tall, light-skinned jeep-driving, music-loving Trinny.

Louis was good to me at first. All we did was party from house to house and drink a lot. He knew everything about me except my age. Looking back, I don't know if he would have cared. He was in his late twenties, maybe thirty. I later found out he was married with kids.

I don't know how he managed to spend so much time with me, but he did. After about three months of partying with Louis, I started to bug him about his wife. I was not the back street kind and I wanted to end it with him.

"You know Louis, you're married."

"So?"

"Well, you don't really think this thing is going to lead any-place? I'm not a back street . . ."

His hand whipped out; the palm stung as it slapped me across the face.

That night, the conversation ended. Over time, he became even more abusive. I was afraid of him and kept trying to duck him. Because of it, I decided it was time to do my hitchhiking act again. But I was not fast enough.

He caught up with me, forced me into his jeep and drove me to the east end of Montreal. A lot of rooming houses were in the east end and the owners didn't ask any questions. Louis had rented a room in one of them for two weeks.

The room he threw me in had a bed, lamp, table and chair. A bare bulb hung from the ceiling and the bathroom was down the hall, a room that I didn't get to for two weeks.

Louis forced drugs on me. I don't know what kind, but they controlled my movements. For added control, he tied my wrists to the old-fashioned bedpost.

For two weeks he raped me over and over. He beat me with a belt, and used a knife to cut tiny slits all over my body, just

41

enough to draw blood. Every two or three days, he brought me food and something to drink, but he wouldn't let me go to the bathroom, so the bed was a mess. That made him angrier and he hurt me even more.

Filled with drugs and fear, I didn't scream. He had complete control of me. Was he going to kill me, I wondered? It did matter. I wanted to die.

After two weeks of hell, he decided not to kill me, at least not there. The last two or three days of my imprisonment, he began acting less savagely. He cleaned me up and put clean sheets on the bed. He placed a bucket in the room for me to use. I could only use it when he was there because he had to untie me. But he came to the room four or five times a day those last days.

"I love you and I'm sorry for what I've done," Louis said. "You know, all of this really is your fault," he continued reasonably. "You've been making me crazy."

The last day, he brought a friend of his, who carried a case of ink and needles. The guy did tattoos. Louis had him tattoo "LOUIS" under my left breast. After the man was finished, he left.

"My friend will say that you came into his tattoo parlor and had him tattoo my name on you because we are so much in love," said Louis. "No one will believe your story about my holding and, uh, hurting you."

Louis untied me. "You're free," he said.

I didn't answer him. I went to the bathroom, had a bath, fixed myself up as best I could and left.

I never asked any of my mob friends to do Louis in. Instead, I got a gun. This was personal.

I spent one month hunting him, but Louis had just disappeared. I never saw him again. I've never stopped looking.

The tattoo is still there.

A few months later, I was arrested for shoplifting and sent to juvenile court again. The judge, who'd seen me before on various minor offenses, was getting tired of my presence.

"Do you have a mother?" he asked me.

"Yes, your honor."

"And what's her name?"

I stopped. What *was* her name? "Well, uh," I stumbled, "her first name is Mary Alice but I don't know her last."

I thought that my grandmother would know about Mary Alice and would give the judge any information he needed to contact her. I was right, and the system found Mary Alice living in a small mining town with her new husband.

She agreed to take me in. She still ran a whorehouse, unknown to the judge, of course.

I took a plane to Alberta where she was now living. After all these years, you might have expected some sort of emotion from her. I was trepiditious and hoping against hope that things might be different.

I didn't know what she looked like any more. A picture of me had been sent to her so she'd recognize me. It was like an immigrant family I knew, where the father had come to the new country and years later, his son joined him. So many years had passed, he had to be introduced to his father on the docks of New York. And then they embraced. I fantasized that would happen to me.

Instead, the two women who walked over were both rip-snorting drunk.

"Dorothy, I'm your mother," said Mary Alice, breathing cheap bourbon into my face. It came out sounding, "Doris, Imma yer muzza."

I kissed her but she didn't kiss me back. I thought of my childhood fantasies of cowboy heroes and hoped they would ride by that night and rescue me.

On the ninety-mile trip back to her home, I rode in the back seat of her Chevy. She and her friend Nancy rode up front. The only words my mother spoke to me as we drove concerned what a jerk my father was. The two women drank from the same bottle and told each other rank jokes. I was not asked anything about myself. I needed to go to the bathroom and I was thirsty, but Mary Alice wouldn't stop the car. I was a cipher, something to be swept aside and ignored.

Home sweet home? Not this one.

My step father, Arthur, was a miner who left for work before light of day and did not return home until after dark in the p.m. I remember him sitting down to eat supper and not saying a word, drinking a bottle of booze, and then going straight to bed.

Weekends were always the same—Arthur and my mother drank and fought. Many times, Mary Alice would run him out of the house at knife point.

I had two half brothers, older than me. Sonny came to visit often. Cappy was married and worked in the mines.

My mother always had a man in the house. For me, there was nothing to do there, just play cards with the men when they came to drink. After awhile, they would go to the bedroom and I would listen to the radio and play solitaire.

One week after I had come "home," Cappy asked me if I wanted to go to town with him, just the two of us. I was happy to go. He was nice to me and it got me out of the house. It was almost sixteen miles to the next town. It was my fifteenth birthday.

Because I only had a few changes of clothes and it didn't seem that Mary was going to buy any for me, my brother Cappy offered to buy me an outfit for my birthday. Everyone went there to shop because it was a much bigger town than ours.

On the way back home, after shopping and dinner, and my brother showing off his new baby sister to his friends, I remember being very happy. Someone loved me.

"I want to take a short cut home," Cappy said, and turned down a side road.

The way he stopped the car a short time later, I thought there was something wrong with the car. I was ready to help my big brother fix it. We were a *team*.

Cappy pulled the car over to the curb and turned out the lights. "Girls earn their way around here, and nothing comes free," Cappy said.

As he talked, I got a sinking feeling.

He got out and pulled me after him. I didn't argue. He pushed me down into the back seat and climbed on top of me.

"You're now a member of the family," Cappy smiled, after he was finished with me. We arrived home and went in together. Cappy looked at Mary Alice. "She's ready," he said simply.

The next day, Mary Alice tried to sell me for twenty dollars to one of her customers. I refused.

During the next weeks, she also tried to sell me to a single miner who was looking for an in-house woman. I was supposed to go live with him. Again, I refused.

While I stayed with her, my mother showed me no love. I ate when she cooked, washed my clothes by hand and tried to stay out of her way. I would take long walks and when I met the local boys, they all laughed at me because I was Mary Alice's daughter. One day, I went out and never went back.

I hitchhiked all the way back to Montreal, over 1,500 miles. I was more restless than ever, hanging around with some middle-class kids. One girl, Carla, said she wanted to run away from home. She came to me because I was the expert on these matters.

At that point, I was thinking of going to Windsor, Ontario, across the border from Detroit. I liked Windsor and Detroit. I met lots of wiseguys there; they worked the border. So we went and wound up in Detroit.

For pleasure, Detroit couldn't be beat. The music industry was hot and the bars always had big name bands. I hung around with singer Sandy Jackson and his guys, in the days before they were famous.

Sandy was a nice guy. I dated him, went to bed with him, but who didn't? He had a lot of women.

I made lots of money running hot goods across the border by boat. My friend had a marina in Windsor where we off-loaded the stuff.

We handled a lot: drugs, leather goods, lots of saddles, and household items. Car parts, you name it, we handled it.

One night, using my Jamaican disguise, I was on my way to the Canadian side of the border to drop off a shipment of stolen auto parts when Carla, who'd been hanging out with some of her friends in Detroit, said that she wanted to tag along. I let her know I was worried about her streets smarts, but decided to let her come anyway.

After I dropped the stuff off and got paid, we decided to hit the road again. Two boys our age, maybe two years older, picked us up in their car. They seemed nice enough, but wild, and we hooked up with them. Their names were Ted and Dan.

Dan had an empty house we could stay in for a few days because his parents were away. We went there. The guys, though, were not what I was used to.

They were *boys*. I had been with grown men all my life. These were just kids looking to party. The party got out of hand.

There was no doubt we had to leave because Ted's parents would soon be home. Dan went out saying, "I'll be back soon." When he returned, it was with a car—not the one he'd been driving, but a new one. He said that it belonged to his uncle.

"My uncle's a real good guy and always let's me use his car," said Dan smoothly. "Do you and Carla want to go with me and Ted to Toronto and find work?"

"Sure," I said. Ditto for Carla.

We left the house taking food and clothes. I noticed Dan putting a rifle in the trunk.

"It's mine and I'm not going to leave it," he explained.

I shrugged. Who cared? We were off to Toronto.

As the miles passed, we started talking about money. The boys were worried. What did we have to sell, how could we live with no money and so on.

"Don't worry," I reassured them. "I have friends in Toronto who will help us, and if push comes to shove, we can work a scam or two until we get jobs."

Just before we hit the border town of Chatem, Ontario, Dan told us about a man who lived in Chatem.

"He keeps big money in his house over the weekend. It's supposed to be money collected from farmers. The money's in a strongbox and the house is easy to rob," he said casually.

At first, Carla and I didn't believe him—it sounded too far out. We just thought he was bragging, trying to impress us.

The wheel shifted back and forth in Ted's hands—Ted was driving—and I realized with a start that they were heading towards this man's house.

Ted and Dan started to plan robbing the guy. They sounded serious. I knew they were for real because I had sat in on plans before. These boys were amateurs, but the pathology was the same as the professional criminals I knew.

I never liked being part of someone else's plans. Carla and I were not asked if we wanted to be part of this score. Usually the men always ask if they should drop the girls off at a motel or truck stop and meet them later, or if they wanted to take part. It was understood that if you took an active part in whatever the deal was, the money was split with all members of the team.

Sometimes I said yes. Sometimes I didn't. This time, I was not asked, and when I brought this to their attention, they said that we could wait in the car.

We arrived at the farmhouse after dark. All the windows were ablaze with light. Ted turned off the car lights when he turned into the long driveway. The pros would have backed into the yard so the getaway would be easier, but not these guys. They were so dense; I started to get worried.

They got out of the car and walked up to the house, looking into all the windows. When they came back, they said they needed our help because there were about four people and if they tried anything, it would be hard to control the situation. I was surprised when Carla agreed.

Never being part of anything like this before, she didn't have a clue as to what she was getting into. It was no more than a joke to her.

I knew different. But I went along with it anyway. I figured I was too far in to chicken out. Wasn't that my reputation? The girl who would go anywhere and dare anything?

There I was, in the middle of an armed robbery. The boys knocked at the back (kitchen) door while we girls stayed a few feet back until the man opened the door. At that time, all of us pushed our way in.

At first, the man thought that we were joking. "A friend of mine set this whole thing up, right?"

"Wrong," Dan said, grim-faced, gazing down the barrel of his rifle that was aimed between the man's eyes. The man quickly realized we weren't friendly.

Dan took man and his wife into the kitchen and kept under control by threatening them with the rifle and loud, bold talk. Then I went into the living room and found two young, teenaged children, a boy and a girl.

"Go into the kitchen and you won't get hurt," I told them firmly. They followed my orders, and then I pulled the telephone out of the wall.

I quickly searched the house for other people.

I was thinking we had been in the house too long; it was dangerous. Someone could have seen us come in. Or maybe a police car going by would see our car, which I suspected was stolen, parked out front.

As if those possibilities were not enough to derail this plan, I found a two-year-old in a crib in the back bedroom. Great. We were dead in the water, but I had to play it out. I went back to the kitchen.

The boys told me to tie the teenagers up back to back and put them on the sofa. As I did this, I asked them if they went to Sunday school.

"Yes," they replied.

"Pray for me," I told them.

Then I brought the baby out into the kitchen to be with his mother; it was warmer in the kitchen and I didn't want anyone to get hurt.

Dan was having a hard time with the man and wanted to tie him up. The boy passed me the gun and I took it without thinking. I stood there pointing the rifle at everyone, more scared than they were, but trying not to show it.

After the man was tied up in such a way that if he moved he would hang himself, I took the baby and put him into the crib that Carla and Ted moved out into the kitchen. After filling the baby's bottle, we started to look for the money.

We searched everywhere but didn't find the big pay off—only a few dollars. After tying up the mother, we made our getaway.

Ted drove quickly. We hit the outskirts of Toronto, and pulled in to gas up. No one came out to the car. So we filled it ourselves. There still was no attendant, so we drive off, thankful for the full tank of free gas.

We drove around Toronto for a few hours looking for some people I knew.

"Oh shit," said Ted.

"What is it?" I said. I looked behind us and saw flashing lights.

Two cops pulled us over. That was it—we were caught!

At the station, I found out what I had suspected: the car was stolen. That's why they pulled us over in the first place. On top of that, the cops already had a report about the robbery. The man and his wife came in and identified us. We were charged with possession of a firearm and car theft, though later I found out the gun legally belonged to Bob.

Eventually, I was also charged with robbery and attempted kidnapping because I handled the baby boy. Despite the fact that I was fifteen at the time, they were going to try me as an adult.

Once again I was back in jail. I looked around my jail cell. I stared at the cold metal bars and the faded bricks, the two tiered bunks covered with blankets, the toilet in the corner, and the sterile cement floor. Unless I could find a way out of this one, I was about to do hard time.

CHAPTER FOUR

Prison

"Miss Mills, do you have anything to say before I pronounce sentence?"

The wrinkle-faced judge sat high and mighty up there on the bench. He looked like an alien in his white wig. But he was about to sentence me to prison. The trial had lasted all of two days; the jury had been out all of two hours, and now I faced two or more years in prison.

I could take it. I had cut my hair and permed it into an afro, putting on some wine-colored makeup in order to look older and tougher. Never mind that I was fifteen going on sixteen; I had legal papers saying that I was eighteen going on nineteen. I got the papers when I first started to run away from home. It didn't hurt to sleep with men in high places and when I got them where I wanted them, they would make changes or amendments to my existing identity. I could get information removed or added depending on my mood and, of course, it would cost me.

"I said Miss Mills, Miss Dorothy Mills, do you have anything to say before I pronounce sentence?"

I shook my head, yet cursed at him under my breath.

"Miss Mills, I sentence you to three years in the Kingston Penitentiary for Women. Maybe that will make a valuable member of society out of you."

"I doubt it," I said with a wan smile, and then I was led out in handcuffs.

As we drove up to the front gate of the Kingston Penitentiary for Women, a chill ran up and down my spine. I stared at the building in front of me: steel bars and limestone walls with rusty barbed wire on top that would cut your skin clean through to the bone. Die from blood loss or lockjaw, take your pick.

All the street stories I'd heard about the prison flashed through my mind. Now I was going to find out the truth first-hand. I looked up at the wire again.

"Oh God, what have I done?" I murmured.

Kingston Prison's large, front double doors opened wide. The outside doors were reinforced steel bars planted in concrete that looked new and strong. The second set of doors was reinforced wood that creaked on its hinges when it was opened by the guards. My escort and I entered the administration section of the prison. It was a veritable bee-hive of activity.

Matrons in white starched pinafores with high, white starched collars and cuffs, strode to and fro in dark blue uniforms. Their stern faces were crowned by close cropped severe haircuts that on the best day would never be called hairstyles. They wore sensible, flat black shoes and walked with their legs tightly held together, as if sticks had been stuck way up their asses. I was surprised to learn that some of these women were married and had children. Their husbands must have used crow-bars in order to keep those legs open long enough to get in there. The kids must have felt like they were being raised by SS guards. But to be fair, a few matrons were very sweet.

They didn't waste anytime in signing me in and taking me for a bath and lice check. Down we went to the basement, where the sounds echoed eerily off the wet, limestone walls. The matron who had become my escort obviously had never heard of electrolysis. She had black hair growing from her chin and thick, black eyebrows growing across her forehead that joined together and came down her nose.

"Strip and get in the tub," her husky voice ordered.

With that, she moved a chair very close to the tub, sat down, crossed her thick, hairy arms and never took her eyes off me. Needless to say, I didn't wash where it was needed, not with *her* watching every move. For all I knew, she was getting off on me.

After toweling off, I was given a blue and white striped, wrap-around frock, the standard prison uniform and turned loose into the general population. As soon as that happened, the next shock hit me—there were men around—it was a coed prison!

Hell, I didn't even know there was such a thing as a coed prison. But why did the men have dresses on? A thought came to me. They were transvestites who had to be kept with the women to keep them safe from the male inmates. That was it.

WRONG!!!

They were not transvestites; they were women. Lesbians, to be more exact.

Now I knew about lesbians. There had been a few in the institutions I passed through, but they were harmless children playing a game of "I'll show you mine if you'll show me yours." A touch and a giggle and that was it. I never had an opinion one way or the other.

Like most of the street people I knew, my attitude was live and let live. We lived with all kinds of mistakes of nature, and every kind of social outcast. So I was not shocked when I realized these "men" were just manly lesbians, but I *was* surprised to see them looking me over. Soon, I realized here was another mine field to get through. It was going to be a challenge.

After I was probed and every orifice of my body looked into for weapons, drugs or any other form of contraband, I was given a uniform and allowed to pass through from the front section of Kingston to the work area. The sewing room was the first place new girls were sent and that's where the guards escorted me. The sewing room was just like the sweat shops I saw in the movies. The room was very large, with rows of out-of-date sewing machines that made the ones used in the Triangle Shirtwaist Company look modern. The largest spools of thread I had ever seen, and big laundry carts overflowing with guards shirts, stood side by side at each machine.

My job was to sew buttons on the epaulets. Sounded simple. Even a monkey could do it. Well, they soon found out I wasn't a monkey because at the end of the day when the finished shirts were counted, it was discovered that in the ones that came from my batch, the buttons were sewn all over the shirts. Others had been sewn together.

"Mills, remove those buttons instantly," the guard ordered me.

"No!" I answered proudly.

That was the end of that. I was given a new job the next day.

Before supper, I was given two sheets, a pillow, one blanket, two towels, one face cloth, one bar of soap, a cup and a Bible. With my arms laden down with these wonderful presents from the state, I was taken to the "range."

"Maybe I'll find my cowboy there?"

What's that you said, Mills?" the guard growled.

"Oh, nothing," I said, stifling a smile and shifting the goods in my arms.

The range was actually the living area where the cells were located. We climbed the stairs and wound up on the second tier, where I was given a cell of my own.

"Now Mills," said the guard, "make your bed. As far as any extras, you can earn some by your work here. We pay three cents a day to every convict that works. Or, you can get help from the outside."

Right, help from the outside. Yeah, sure.

There was not going to be any help from the outside; so I would work and make the three cents a day.

"When Canteen Day comes around once a month, you can buy any extras you need. Now get your cell ready, because we eat in five minutes," the guard continued.

Five minutes later, the guards escorted us to the dining room for supper. Everyone was watching me. I sat down at a table with two other women. One, Alice, a lady with a round, cherubic face and graying hair in bun, was about sixty-years-old. She was in for performing an abortion. The second woman, Margarita, was petite with her wavy brown hair caught in a ponytail, about thirty. She'd committed some sort of fraud. Neither talked much after telling me their names and offenses. That was fine with me.

After dinner, the sour-faced matron gave me a stiff cotton night gown and I went to bed. I was just starting to doze off when I heard disco music and loud talking.

"Yeah, what the fuck we need that for?."

"Shit, I don't know. This is great, right?"

It came from the lower level, just under me. When I looked over the rail outside my cell, there were at least six girls dancing. And they were all drunk. Now how could that be? Home brew, I was to find out later.

I also found out later that the matrons would stay away from the area when these parties were going on. As long as everyone would go in their cells at lock up, the guards would not be called.

One of the partying convicts saw me.

"Come on down here, nigger, and show us how to dance," she shouted up at me.

"I can't dance and don't call me nigger."

She had a stupid, drunken smile on her face that I wanted to pound into oblivion. I imagined her teeth shattering like so many broken china plates.

"Hell, I'm only calling you what you are. Besides, all niggers can dance."

We argued back and forth like that until a matron got worried, because she could hear all six girls threatening to beat me up and me threatening to kill them all. The matron walked over and stood outside the gate until lock down to make sure nothing bad happened.

The next day, the convicts were too hung over from the night before to worry about me. In the days that followed, that same woman who started the argument with me came to respect me enough to leave me alone. She was some heavy drug lady on the streets in Vancouver, but she was also a user and because of that, she would get careless sometimes and get busted. This was the second time in Kingston Prison for her.

The first time around, she got out early for good behavior. This second time the judge had given her two and a half years, but she would never serve all of that. Junkie girls never finished their time. Society didn't look at them as a major menace. That's why, unless they messed up on the inside and wound up in the hole for something like operating a still, they could expect to get out early. Also, they were never without drugs. Drugs were sent into them in a variety of ways, but one of the most popular is what I dubbed Special Delivery.

A letter would be sent to them in code (to get by the censors) ahead of time, so they would know what day to expect the drop. Then, on the appointed day, they'd hang out by the wall at night. Suddenly, a package would come sailing over the wall. They'd pick it up and find their dope inside.

Another good way to get what they needed was to have a matron bring the stuff in for her "special friend." These are only a few of the many ways to get drugs inside the prison.

Anyway, my nemesis Frankie, the dealer/junkie from Vancouver, seemed to hold some power in Kingston at that time and after realizing that she could not get me to over to her side, she grudgingly backed off.

I had never belonged to a gang on the street, and I wasn't going to start just because I was behind bars. I couldn't handle the discipline or the responsibility of being part of a group. Even in prison, I was a free bird.

Frankie was different; she'd adjusted well to prison and lived well on the inside. She received the most mail. Holiday packages full of goodies, all kinds of stuff that she shared with the other inmates. Not me, except when she left.

The day she left, the matron called me aside.

"Frankie left this for you."

It was a box and a note. The note read:

"Niggers love music. Have fun."

Frankie had left me her records.

Unlike the men's pen, the gays ran the women's joint. They were the biggest and the baddest. The Butch Broads made slaves out of some of the younger girls. They saw me with my big breasts and trim, strong body and figured I was like the rest. It was Bertha the Butch who caused me trouble.

Bertha was the baddest and the biggest. She had broad shoulders, was close to six feet with close-cropped blond hair and a mad on for anyone and anything.

"Hey Babe, where you from?" she asked me one day in the yard during exercise period.

"Montreal," I said.

"I hear the chicks in Montreal suck pussy."

"This chick don't," I said and walked away.

She kept that up for a week or so, taunting me, asking me if I liked sucking pussy and how if I didn't she'd get me to like it.

"Get lost," I kept telling her, but Bertha couldn't. She had a reputation to uphold.

During the second week, she managed to push me a few times when we were in line, and when we came back from mess. I ignored her, until finally, one day, she pushed me hard enough that I hit a cell on the second tier. This was just after lunch and right before lock down. I saw red.

I launched off the wall and plunged my head into her stomach. As the breath was knocked out of her, she cried "Oomph." She deflated like a flattened balloon but kept her footing. With my head in her stomach, I threw punches at her flanks, hoping to damage her kidneys and make the fight end fast. She pushed me off and banged my head against the wall. I scratched at her eyes.

By then, the prisoners were cheering, but I didn't know for whom—and I didn't care. I kicked out. She caught my leg and spun me around. As I fell, her foot came toward my face. When it came down, it found air. I reached over, pulled her leg toward me and bit her hard in the ankle like Gabby Hayes did to so many villains in cowboy movies.

"Owww," she yelled and pulled free from my jaws.
I got up and kicked her in the groin. Her face tightened in pain and she went down on all fours. I came up from the floor with an uppercut and her head jerked back from the punch. She was semi-conscious now and I wasn't thinking, just reacting.

I pulled her up and dragged her over to the railing on the second tier. I was just getting her legs over the top bar when the guards came rushing and restrained me. It took four of them. Kicking and screaming, I tried to get away. They picked me up and carried me downstairs to a holding cell.

I was the new chick on the block. Nobody, including the guards, wanted to hear that I'd bucked the order of things. Bertha the Butch and her band of merry women ran things and it wasn't good for the status quo if I came along and ruined them. So I got sentenced to the hole for fifty-two days of bread and water.

The hole. The hole was a subterranean area where six cells had been carved into the limestone floors. Three had toilets, the others a hole in the floor and no sink to wash up in. And no light. I had the privilege of a toilet. At first.

I blocked it with my underwear and used it as much as possible. The next morning when the matron came down with my bread and water and waited to take my tin cup from the night before, I gave it to her all right—in the face with my body wastes. I laughed as it dripped off her. Every opportunity I had, I gave everyone a hard time.

That was the end of my toilet era. They transferred me to the next cell and thereafter, I had to squat on the bare, stone floor over a hole, making sure my aim was accurate because if I missed, I had to clean it up. You could hear the shit hit with a plunk in the underground cesspool. Every day and night, a foul odor came up through that hole. In time, I learned to tolerate it and eventually, ignore it.

The only way to tell the time of day when you were in the hole was, if you strained against bars. Then you might see a shaft of sunlight filtering in to the room, piercing the darkness of the dungeon-like space. The only light came from a dim light bulb, covered by a grate that had been implanted in the ceiling.

Every three days, by law, I had to be given one boiled potato and a bowl of mush. The only reading material I was allowed was the Bible. The Bible had been used on me and against me all my life. I was not impressed.

Nothing to do. Day after day after day. No exercise, except pacing my cell, which took all of two seconds one way and two seconds the other. After awhile, I started singing.

I sang at the top of my lungs. In my head, I was on a stage in a beautiful gown, hypnotizing my adoring audience with a voice not unlike the great Lena Horne or Billie Holiday, or maybe I was a classical diva like Leontyne Price. The cell was large enough to swing my arms around and do a kick but not large enough to do many steps. So I danced on the same spot.

I was all alone, isolated and except for my fantasy. There was no escape. After awhile, I was visited upon by the demons of the past. By this time, I couldn't tell day from night, I couldn't tell what was real and what wasn't. After long sessions of cursing and boxing the air, I would collapse from extreme exhaustion.

After fifty-two days, when I was released from the hole and back into the general prison population, I finally saw daylight. It didn't last long. I fought viciously with the other prisoners. The matrons would not touch me. They sent for guards from the men's side across the street to handle me. Three to four large men took me, kicking and screaming, all the way to the hole. But even they had a hard time with me.

When one guard tried to subdue me and escort me to the subterranean depths, I put my head between his legs and bit his balls. He never came back.

Kingston Prison was a circus, and I was the ringmaster. Those first six months, I spent at least half the time down in the hole with my demons. But I wouldn't let them win. Soon, I had them jumping through hoops like everyone else who messed with me.

After many fights, most of which I won, the lesbians finally left me alone. Betty the Butch and her friends were big, but they had gone to pot. I was in very good shape, very strong and when I hit somebody, they stayed down.

I danced every day, ran up and down stairs, and out-crazied all of them. Everyone believed I was mad. I trashed my cell, broke windows, spat in the matrons face, beat up inmates and broke every rule in the place and some they had never conceived of. Finally, I proved to them I was a true incorrigible. Enter the prison psychiatrist, Dr. George Kaveneaugh.

One day I was taken to Dr. Kaveneaugh's office. It was institutional green, not unlike any of the other offices in the prison, with a plain, simple mahogany desk. Dr. Kaveneaugh was in his early fifties, with wispy brown hair, overweight, and wore a simple suit and white shirt with tie. He might have been someone's grandfather: he had that type of kindly expression permanently affixed on his face.

"Dorothy, I'm going to ask you a lot of questions about your childhood and I want you to answer them as truthfully as possible. And I promise you, no more going to the hole."

That was it. That was all I had to hear. For the first time in who knew how long, someone was respecting me enough to make a deal. I did as he asked and told him everything about my background. Why not? With the hole out of the way, I had nothing to be afraid of.

Shortly after the assessment from Dr. Kaveneaugh, along came the man with the little black box.

"Dorothy, we have this treatment, which'll make you feel better," Dr. Kaveneaugh began. And then he proceeded to tell me about shock treatments. What did I know? I was an uneducated street kid. Out of ignorance and curiosity, I agreed, and signed a paper to that effect.

I was taken to a room set aside for such treatments next to the prison infirmary. The prison nurse wordlessly strapped me to a hospital bed, both legs and arms, and a fifth strap held my head down. Sodium pentothal was injected into my arm.

"Begin counting backwards from one-hundred," said the nurse.

In walked a short man holding a little black box.

"One hundred, ninety-nine, ninety-eight," I counted, wondering exactly what the black box was for, "ninety-seven, ninety-six, ninety-five, ninety-four, ninety-three, ninety-two, ninety-one...." and off I went into another world.

I have no idea what happened to me while I was unconscious and helpless, but I do know that when I awakened back in my cell, my arms and legs twitched uncontrollably and I had a terrific headache. It felt like someone was inside my head with jackhammers going at full trip. I do know that I didn't want to see the man or his black box again. But like so much in my life, what I wanted didn't matter. I had signed a document giving them the

61

right to do I don't know what to me, and I had been forced into a "treatment plan" against my will.

Time after time, I was taken to that room off the infirmary, injected with truth serum and made to count backwards. And time after time, the man and his black box wordlessly entered. And time after time, as I collapsed into unconsciousness, I screamed but no sound came out of my mouth. And when I awoke, it was with a tremble and a shudder and a dread that would not go away.

As for my attitude, there were no visible improvements. Why should there be? They were torturing me against my will the same way my parents and cousins and the rest of my miserable family had.

Eventually, seeing no improvement, they stopped the shock treatments. I was left with a big pentothal habit. I would faint all over the place, cry and cry. I went back to stuttering.

They gave me a respite of a few months, during which I kicked pentothal cold. Meanwhile, I began cutting up again and making a general nuisance out of myself. Since shock treatments and isolation didn't break my spirit, the prison doctors were trying to figure out what to try next.

In Hollywood sanitariums at that time, a drug called L.S.D. was being used as a treatment for unruly patients. The reports said that many actors and actresses were being helped. In Canada, the drug was still in the experimental stages and inmates were being used as guinea pigs to gauge the short and long range effects. Because of my record, I was chosen to be one of the main test animals.

Dr. Mark Eveson was the doctor who administered the drug to me. The first time, he overdosed me by accident. Five days later, I was still on a trip without any luggage. After that, I took many trips, most of them rather pleasant, though they did not last as long as the first.

While I was becoming an acid head, things in Kingston Prison went on as usual. I had not settled down or in. I had served about one year when I figured out how to survive the lesbians. I would join them.

There was a small group of women—timid, weak-minded and docile—who were constantly preyed-upon by the Butches. The only crime these women had committed was listening to and following their men. Going on bank jobs, breaking and enterings, paper hanging (forging checks), crimes like that. They were neither smart nor tough. So I decided to take them over.

For a price, we agreed that I would pretend to be their "special" friend. That's how I became "Big Daddy" to four or five women—the numbers would change as people left and new ones came in. To play the role well, I cut my hair shorter and swaggered around like a rooster in a hen house. It was the first time in the history of the prison that a female inmate had a stable. I was the talk of the joint. I had out-butched the Butches.

For the favor of providing the weak protection from the rest, the women made sure my clothes were washed and ironed, my cell was cleaned and spotless. They knitted me socks and shared their canteen goods with me. I also got all the butts I could smoke. Cigarettes are as good as money in prison, and I had one of the more lucrative bank accounts.

All in all it was a great act. My cover was never blown, and a whole group of women did their time without being violated.

Meanwhile, the L.S.D. treatments continued. I went all over the universe, unfortunately without leaving Kingston. Dr. Eveson turned out to be okay and we became friends but he did not hold out too much hope for me with the L.S.D. treatment. It seemed that nothing worked on me. Big surprise! In my eyes, I was okay. My problem was prison. No one liked that.

The difference between me and everybody else was I showed my anger, big time. Even though I had practically grown up in institutions, I was damned if I would become institutionalized. No one, *no one* was going to break me.

By then, I had pulled so many scams in Kingston Prison that there was not much left to try. Only one thing was left—escape. It had never been done from the woman's side. Well, I figured, there always has to be a first time.

CHAPTER FIVE

Escape from Kingston

"Hey, Dorothy, you're up!"

I didn't hear anything. I dreamed of a safe life, far away, free from perversion.

"Hey Dorothy, you're up," Sheila repeated.

I opened my eyes.

The first thing I saw was the latticed underside of the bench that the ball players were sitting on. The hot, summer sun was still beating down, but I was no longer thousands of miles away in my daydreams. I was sprawled on the grass behind the first base dugout.

"Let's go, young lady," shouted the umpire, who was actually one of the guards.

I grabbed a bat and trotted toward homeplate, eyeing the placement of the infielders. Sometimes it was policewomen's teams that came in to play us, sometimes a local pickup team from the town of Kingston. Today, it was the cops.

Usually, they brought treats to us and today was no exception. We feasted on a diabetic's fantasy of candy, chewing gum and soda. There was always enough to go around; they were so nice to us on the inside, yet on the outside, they did everything they could to put us away. It didn't make sense.

"Strike one!" shouted the umpire.

The ball had sailed in without my seeing it. I was still daydreaming. Needed to concentrate. I wasn't any all-star player, but

I could hit the ball pretty good when I wanted. There were runners on second and third. With two out, a clutch hit was needed to bring 'em home.

"Strike two" The ball smacked into the catcher's glove.

"Whaddaya mean a strike?" I turned and shouted at the umpire. "It barely hit the outside corner."

"Ms. Mills would you like to keep batting or go back to your cell?"

I never took crap from anybody, but I enjoyed being outside. The last thing I needed was to go back into that dank dungeon that I called home. I needed to choke down my anger before I let it fuck me up again.

I stepped out of the box and looked around. All I noticed was the bench and the players sitting on it. I stepped back in. The pitcher wound up and the ball went whistling through the air. I pulled the bat back to the cocked position, and stepped forward.

"Strike three, take a seat," the ump shouted—I could swear he was smiling under that mask—as my bat continued to sail through the strike zone without touching the whirling sphere.

Strangely, I didn't care that I'd struck out. I looked back at the bench. Something about it seemed to transfix me . . . .

Half an inning later, I was back lying down on the grass when it came our turn to bat. From that position, I looked upside down at the bottom of the bench again. It had large crossboards that looked strong enough to climb if turned over. The bench itself looked like it was about seven feet long. It was then I conceived my plan to bust out of Kingston Prison.

Turning, the prison wall rose up in front of me, about twenty feet high. Above that was ten more feet of steel fence going straight up, topped off by another foot of rusty barbed wire whose prickly thorns slanted up at sharp angles.

I squinted into the midday sun. Shouldn't be any problem, I was thinking, not with a prison blanket to take care of the barbed wire. They were woven so tightly and from such tough cloth that nails had a hard time penetrating the fibers. So that took care of that. Next up was positioning. I looked up and around.

There were no guard towers on the woman's side of the prison. No dogs patrolling the perimeter. No regular outside patrols. These guys were crazy. Did they think they could keep women locked up behind bars without one even attempting an escape with such lousy security? What gall men sometimes have when evaluating women's abilities.

Many women actually have it better in jail than on the outside. But for me, freedom has always been the most important thing.

The drug experiments and the electric shocks. The hole where you couldn't see daylight. Having to pose as a lesbian with my own stable of chicks in order to avoid fights. I couldn't bear any more of that crap.

During exercise period, prison rules allowed us to take blankets out to sit on; they were counted. No problem. The next day, I secretly put one blanket inside the other. The matron assumed I was only taking out one blanket. Meanwhile, I hid the second one in the tall grass behind third base.

I had supper and returned to my cell as I always did. Nothing out of the routine. The cell door was left open until lights out, which was ten p.m.

Quickly, I stuffed two pillows under the bedcovers to shape a body, and turned my cell light off. Now, the dim corridor bulb cut a shaft of life through my cell. It fell on the mound on the bed that looked exactly like a prisoner huddled under the covers. I smiled and softly closed my cell door behind me.

Taking care to avoid contact with inmates and guards alike, I emerged into the darkness like a caterpillar from its cocoon. Shadows had lengthened on the baseball diamond. Third base beckoned. The blanket was still there when I went to retrieve it. Good. It never occurred to me that anyone would find it. But now for the more difficult part.

Man! I was a strong kid, but it was hard work dragging that heavy black bench across the yard over two hundred feet to the blind corner.

Dressed in street clothes—we could change into street clothes after work—I leaned the bench up against the wall and climbed the slats, with my blanket firmly in tow. It was a reach but I managed to get to the small lip on top of the stone wall. I pushed the bench back; it landed in the tall grass where it would not easily be discovered. Now to get over the fence and wire.

The fence was no problem. I just climbed. At the top, I looked at the prickly barbed wire thorns and smiled. "Fuck you," I mumbled. Putting the blanket over the wire, I hoisted myself over. The blanket did its job; though I could feel their sharpness through the fabric, the barbs did not penetrate.

Now I was poised on the lip of the wall on the far side. Just room enough for the toes on my feet to rest. Thank god I have a small shoe size. I pulled at the blanket to free it from the wire, and turned it catty-cornered so that I could get maximum length out of it. As I had nothing on the outside to get down on, I wove a corner of the blanket in among the chain link, and shinnied down the blanket to the very end.

There I was hanging in space. I looked down. It was a long jump because the ground on the outside was lower than the inside. What the hell—I let go of the blanket and jumped. With all the exercise, my legs had become powerful, the muscles thick and strong, and they took the brunt of the fall. I landed like a cat.

I didn't move for a while, waiting for my heart to stop pounding. I could swear the guards would hear the insistent rhythms, so loud were they in my chest. When I felt comfortable enough to move, I sprang to my feet and crossed the deserted street that ran in front of the prison. It's a good thing there wasn't a full moon, because the moonlight would have glinted off my self-satisfied grin as I strolled right past the front gate.

After about ten blocks, I started to hitchhike. I avoided cars—only a truck would do. I knew truckers. I knew what I could get out of them. Soon, a truck caught me in its headlights, and braked. The passenger side door opened.

"Goin' as far as Montreal," the trucker said with an easy smile.

Montreal. Home ground. Just the name was music to my ears.

"Great!" I could barely contain my joy.

"Well, what you waitin' for? Hop in."

And hop in I did. I knew we would be in Montreal before the guards even discovered I was missing and the alarm went out. The police would not know until later because the prison officials would be busy looking for me inside the compound. It would take over an hour to search the ducts and underground tunnels. That's where they would figure I would have gone. Then they would search the grounds inside the walls, probably another hour before the blanket was discovered on the ground outside the wall and after that, the bench in the tall grass. All in all, about a twelve hour head start.

"My name's Harlan, what's yours?" the trucker said brightly.

"Prince," I answered. "Diana Prince."

I don't know why I said that. Probably because that was "Wonder Woman's" secret identity, and "Wonder Woman" had been one of my idols growing up. She was powerful, a good guy with strength and substance, the type of person I longed to be. But that was fantasy.

"Wonder Woman," was a super heroine who traveled in an invisible plane with her lover, "Steve Trevor." Me, I was an escaped convict hitching a ride in a dirty semi with a rumpled trucker.

The headlights picked up the winding white line of the two-lane blacktop, leading down an endless road into a distant future. Good. Let the future stay out there for a while. I sat back in the truck and huddled in the warmth of the heater, staring out at the abstract shapes of trees and buildings and bushes and barns that swept by in the darkness.

I closed my eyes. Soon, I was winging off into the clouds with my lover.

The sun came in through the slatted blinds. It felt warm and comforting on my face. I opened my eyes, expecting to be on a Caribbean island with Steve Trevor. Instead, I saw the trucker's nude, hairy body in the bed next to mine.

The room was plainly furnished. We were in one of the working sections of Montreal. We had gone there after getting to the city in the early hours of the a.m.

"Why don't you come home with me? That is, if you need a place to stay," Harlan had said.

If I had anything, why would I be dressed so shabbily and hitching? So I went back to his place, hoping he wasn't going to be some deviant who'd hand me my ass on a platter.

That night, I was lucky again. It had actually been rather pleasant, making love to a guy after being in prison with all those bull dykes. Afterwards, Harlan fell asleep and a short time later, so did I.

After we got up the next morning Harlan turned the radio on.

Last night, a female convict escaped from Kingston Penitentiary. Dorothy Elizabeth Mills is nineteen, described by authorities by being five feet two inches tall, weight one hundred and ten pounds. She has a coffee-colored complexion. She is believed to have escaped by way of a secret tunnel that goes under the prison. If you have any information as to her whereabouts, there is a reward for information. Contact your local RCMP detachment if you have information.

We both laughed at the same time.

"What a hoot," said Harlan. "And we went right by that place. Can you believe that?"

"Oh yeah," I said laughing too, "I can believe it. Boy, can I!"

But I was laughing for a different reason than he was.

Obviously, the white authorities did not know how to describe a person of multiracial background. Not only had I effected the first ever escape from Kingston, the cops had given the media a totally erroneous description of me. The only thing that was correct was my sex. I've never been "coffee-colored" in my life, even with a tan. I was 5'6 1/2". The afro perm had grown out by now, and I made a mental note to dye my hair as soon as possible. I also had the largest hooters that I've ever seen on a young girl.

"Boy, that's something," Harlan laughed again. "I'm lucky that I didn't pick that chick up, eh?"

"Oh, yes," I answered earnestly.

"Yeah," Harlan continued, "those women in prison are rough. You know, bet if I'd picked up that wild girl, she woulda stabbed me and stolen my rig."

I would have given anything to see the look on his face when he found out who I was. Later that day, I saw the article about me in the local newspaper. It was wire service copy that was picked up and printed all over the country, and read:

Seventeen-Year-old Girl Fools Pen Guards; Escapes Kingston

KINGSTON, Ont. (CP) - Dorothy Elizabeth Mills, seventeen-year-old fugitive from Kingston penitentiary women's prison, fooled guards making a Sunday night cell check by stuffing a dummy into her bed. The girl pushed two pillows under bed covers to shape a body and lowered herself over a prison wall with a blanket.

Her escape, first in the history of Canada's federal prison for women, was not discovered until morning, after a groundsman noticed the hanging blanket. Police believe she escaped following the evening recreation period. They think she carried a ladder to a point out of sight of the guard house, used it to scale the wall, then lowered herself down the other side.

Born in Dominion, N.S., Miss Mills was sentenced last March to three years in prison for robbery and auto theft.

I closed the newspaper. I knew that the police would not be able to pick me up from the identification that they had, so I was comfortable walking around town.

I got in touch with some old friends. Pocket money was what I needed. Hell, I didn't want to commit any crimes. Just have 'em lend me some money, enough to get by on.

"Hello, Jeannie? This is Chickie."

"Jake, yeah it's Chickie. Yeah, I know. Long time, no see. Where have I been? Well, sort of busy."

All I wanted was to taste the freedom again of the open road, to drive for miles and miles across Canada and the United States and never stop. Most of all, to get away from all those damn women! At least for a little while—who cared if they caught me in a week or two as long as I had my break?

But I was not about to make it easy on the authorities, so I changed my looks again. I got a straight, black-haired wig, used makeup to emphasize my slightly almond-shaped eyes, and hung around Montreal for a few weeks, sleeping in a different place every night. Every day I passed the police and even chatted with the beat cops in Chinatown. They didn't even blink.

After I raised almost a thousand dollars, I headed out on the road again. This time, I crossed the border at Windsor, and went to my old haunt in Detroit. From there, I made it to Chicago. Once again, I changed my identity, this time by dyeing my hair red and using my Scottish accent.

Chicago is a great town to walk in. It's like a miniature version of New York, but without the garbage. I had walked all through the downtown area.

Hardly noticing that day had turned into night, I found myself in a very dark place. Now I looked around. I saw very wide streets and a few street lights. The place seemed deserted. No people. There were sidewalks, but there were no buildings flush with them. It was all open space and silhouettes of warehouse-shaped buildings in the distance. Echoes of junkyard dogs' barking did not add to my feelings of comfort.

Not much traffic, mostly trucks and all going the opposite way from me. I was hungry and very tired. I didn't want to get stuck walking around this part of Chicago all night and I didn't want to sleep in an open field. I decided to hitchhike.

Suddenly, an old clunker of a car stopped a few yards ahead of me. Most of the time, I stayed away from cars and tried to ride in trucks. But now there was no one else around. I approached the vehicle warily.

"Hello, there," said the driver in a soft, calming voice.

His appearance made me feel a little easier. He was red-headed, slightly lighter than the shade I'd picked for my hair, and about forty with a big, wide smile. I was immediately disarmed.

"How are you tonight, young lady?" The slight burr of his accent was familiar.

I told him I was hungry and had no place to sleep.

"Well, I can help you fix that," he continued in that soft burr. "I'll take you to my older sister's house. You'll be looked after."

He didn't say anything else. The choice was mine. His smile became even wider when I got into the car and closed the door.

"Oh, you're going to love my sister."

"What's your name sir?"

"It's Ian, Ian Black. And you're . . . ?"

"Mary. That's a nice name, Ian. You're a Scotsman, aren't you?" I asked, matching his accent burr for burr. He nodded, then went back to the subject of his sister.

"My sister's a great cook," Ian continued. "You know, she and I spent most of our childhoods right around here, when it was still a good neighborhood with good, kind people."

"Oh really?"

"Yes, it was such a nice place to grow up. The boys played stoop ball every day and the girls skipped rope, they used two of them—what did they call it . . . "

"Double Dutch," I answered smiling. "I did that back home."

"Right. Double Dutch. It was such a good time . . . ." He looked over at me. "You're Scottish, too, aren't you?"

I smiled, "You noticed."

"My sister will like that."

As we drove, he told me more stories about his youth, of rooting for the Cubs—which was such futile pursuit since they hadn't won a pennant since 1919, of summers swimming down by the lake and, sometimes, sneaking into the private beaches up in Highland Park.

Of these illicit adventures he said, "The people there, they couldn't tell whether we were rich like them or poor. I guess you can't tell the difference when someone's in a swimsuit," and we both laughed at that.

Ian looked over at me. Some people are very simpatico. They just pick up on things real quick, like they're psychic. Ian seemed to know just what would get to me. Or maybe it was just that he smelled the desperation and fear.

"But I tell you, there were a lot of bad things happening in my home and even my sister couldn't protect me. No one could. So you know what?"

"What?"

"I took to the road." He looked over at me again. "I suppose I was about your age. And I traveled all over this great country."

He didn't know I was on the lam from prison in Canada. But he'd guessed enough to know that if I hadn't had problems, I wouldn't have been out so late at night, all alone in the wrong part of town.

I don't remember what story I told him about myself, about being in trouble. There were so many that I'd made up, I could choose from them like a library when the need arose. Whatever I said, he was willing to help me.

By the time we arrived at Ian's big sister's home, I was twice as hungry after being seduced by his wonderfully folksy stories of her fabulous cooking. With his colorful tales and my vivid imagination, my mouth was watering.

Big sister lived in a strange building that stood alone on a block that had ben razed to topsoil. It looked like parts of New York City, so its appearance did not surprise me. The people living in the building must have been very poor, but that did not matter to me. I had eaten many a good meal at a poor man's table.

We parked—there was no problem getting a space—and I followed him inside. I didn't realize how big he was until we got out of the car. He was at least 6'2" and 200 pounds. It was a very warm night, but yet he had a jacket on.

Inside, we walked towards the stairs, then went down to the basement and ended up in a labyrinth. There were rooms and pipes and corridors and after a few seconds going this way and that, I knew that I could never find my way out alone. Water dripped someplace, over and over, echoing. No windows, only a bare light bulb here and there, creating pools of light and in between, shadows out of which crawled an occasional rat.

A sour smell assaulted my nostrils as I walked through the labyrinth with this man who called himself Ian Black. He had been talkative in the car, but now he had suddenly grown quiet.

He stopped before a grey, metallic door. His knock reverberated down the corridor and sent chills up my spine and made me want to run. He had laid a restraining arm across my back, and I knew that escape would be impossible. The door opened.

She could have easily been "The Wicked Witch of the West." Her hard, ugly face was partially obscured by strands of dirty blond hair and she was drunk. Saying nothing, the woman looked at me through empty, watery blue eyes, turned and walked back to the chair she had been sitting on, sat down and continued to smoke and drink out of a bottle. On a table in front of her was a messed up newspaper and a deck of greasy cards. She never looked up when the man put a folded five dollar bill on top of the cards.

It had all happened so fast. By the time "Ian" took my hand and pulled me into another room with a curtain for a door, I knew I was trapped. There was a bed, a chair and a crate that substituted for a night table. A very dim light was on, but not dim enough to hide the dirt. The place was a pig sty, as squalid as anything I had ever seen.

My false savior towered over me. He was tall when stretched to his full height and I had to look up to see his face.

"Strip now," was all he said. The words were said in the same, soft voice, the smile was just as effusive and yet, I knew that if I tried to resist, the smile would stay, the voice would get softer and I would be dead. I didn't even try to resist.

He lay down on the bed, his weight sagging the mattress and springs to the floor. The sheets were so dirty they were stiff.

"Sit on my face," he ordered.

My heart was beating faster, the adrenaline kicking in, my body close to shock. Did he say sit on his face or *shit* on his face? I was familiar with both requests.

"Would you please say that again, I—"

The flap of his jacket flipped back and out of a shoulder holster he whipped as large a Bowie knife as I had ever seen.

"That's the first time I've ever seen a knife holster—"

He put the knife to my vagina and pulled my face into his lap, where I sucked his penis until he told me to stop. Then he placed the knife against my throat and pumped me a few times, in and out. My mind drifted back to someplace, hoping "Wonder Woman" would break in and save me, or maybe if I believed hard enough, "Superman" would exist and he'd break through the walls . . .

"Now I want you to piss on me."

The knife was held against my ass and he pressed it just a little way up my rectum. I was so nervous, I didn't know if I could urinate, but the stream finally came and he turned his face up against it with a beatific smile.

It went on like that for I don't know how long, until his demons had been satiated. Then he hustled me out through the corridors and out to the street. I don't know how long he had abused me. It was still night and still warm, but the warm, stagnant air felt like a refreshing breeze on my face.

I was still dazed when he put me in his car and drove me to the outskirts of the city. I guess he did that because he didn't want me to remember where the apartment building was. He didn't know it wouldn't have made a difference. I couldn't call the cops.

"See you again," he said with his soft voice and warm smile, and then the Scotsman-from-hell drove away.

Across the street was an oasis of light, an all-night gas station. I wandered over and into the bathroom on the side. A bare bulb hanging from the ceiling provided a harsh light. I stared at myself in the bathroom's shattered mirror. I was surprised to see that I didn't look any different than I usually did, with the exception of the fact that I had just been raped at knifepoint and almost killed.

I got myself cleaned up as best I could and hitched a ride with a trucker. No more cars for me. Ever.

After about ten, long-distance rides, I found myself back in Montreal. Now what to do? I had two half-brothers who lived in Alberta. Cappy I didn't want to see, but the other one I was sure would help me.

I got on the road again with another trucker, hitching rides until I got to Alberta province. On the Trans Canada Highway, we rode over the Bow River and into Calgary, where I got off. After asking around, I found out that my brother was in East Coulee, staying at my mother's house. I hadn't seen either of them for what seemed like ages.

East Coulee, ninety miles east of Calgary, is a small mining village with wooden sidewalks and nearby foothills, built on the banks of the Red Deer River. The mines were on the west side of town. There was one road in and one road out.

It's the type of town best passed through at night. Seen in the low beams of your headlights, it looks like any sleepy river town, once seen and soon forgotten. During the day, though, you can see the desperation that flakes off the unpainted, ramshackle houses that flank the stagnant waters of the Red Deer River, and the depressing faces of the town's 683 inhabitants who have little to hope for in life besides finding a way out of East Coulee.

"Hello, Sonny?"

I was phoning from a gas station, the only one in town.

"Dorothy?"

"Yes, it's me, Sonny."

"Oh, Dorothy, you all right, eh? We heard about your escape."

"I'm fine."

"Look Dorothy, why don't you come to my place. Mary Alice's away so you won't have to deal with her."

"That's a good idea." I was so relieved. I could rest up and make a plan. Sonny would help me.

He gave me the address and I walked over. Sonny greeted me with a kiss and a bearhug.

"Oh, Dorothy, I'm so glad to see you."

"Me too, Sonny," I grinned.

He took me inside and made dinner, steak with all the trimmings, with bottles and bottles of Canadian beer, the real thing.

"Dorothy," Sonny said as he chewed, "if you get a job and stay out of trouble for about three years, the authorities'll give up looking for you."

That sounded good.

"But whatever, okay, look, *whatever* you want to do, I'll back you."

"That makes me feel so good, so good, better than I've felt—"

I looked up as the screen door banged shut.

"So what's all this?" an seldom heard but familiar voice called out.

I stood up, shocked and surprised, then looked back at my brother, who shrugged his shoulders.

"Hello, Mum," I said.

"Well, Dorothy, this is a surprise. Come to visit your family?"

As I looked at her, I smelled those same antiseptic smells from those long ago winter days in her parlor and felt cramps from deep inside my body.

Mary Alice didn't join us, preferring to hit the bottle. Nothing had changed. After she got drunk, she started to get mean. Like I said, nothing had changed.

"Why don't you do something with your life?" she shouted at me. "Instead of being a criminal!"

She frightened the hell out of me. I was afraid I'd kill her in self defense. I just took it and fought back the tears. I wouldn't give her the satisfaction of seeing me cry.

I took my brother into the kitchen.

"I can't stay in this house with her. I hate her guts. What about California? Yeah, that's it. I'll go out there."

"That doesn't sound like such a bad idea, kid."

My brother began to give me directions to the West Coast, what highways to take and such. I sensed that someone else was there. It was my mother again, standing at the doorway.

"How much have you heard?" I asked.

"Enough," she answered, a note of compassion creeping into her voice. "Look, why don't you wait until I get some money from the hotel. See, I know the owner and he'll cash my check any time. I'm one of the important people in this town," she told me proudly. "After all, you'll need some money to get out of town and I can get it for you," she urged.

I looked at my brother, who nodded quickly. I decided I had to trust her. I would have been a fool to try and escape over the foothills without a guide and a pack. The river was out of the question and hiding in an abandoned mine shaft was not my idea of freedom. Yes, Mary Alice was my only hope.

I was bone tired. I didn't want to go through what I'd gone through in Chicago again. I wanted enough money so at least I'd have a place to sleep and something to eat on the road.

"Okay," I finally agreed. "I'll wait for you here."

Less than an hour later, the kitchen door crashed open and RCMP officers burst through with drawn guns.

My trust had been misplaced.

"You won't need those," I said quietly, sipping my coffee at the kitchen table.

The twilight was pierced by the headlights of the police cars, lights that were aimed into the front room of the house. They were using their high beams as searchlights. It was all rather theatrical—another bloody movie in the starring vehicle that was my lousy life.

If my mother had been a law abiding, moral and socially correct woman who turned me in for my own good, I could understand her actions. But she turned me in for nothing but the bounty money.

What I saw in the short time I was there let me know that Mary Alice had not changed. She was still a whore, still a bootlegger, still a procurer of other women. Greed and lust were her only allies. She had never made a kind gesture on my behalf and this was no exception.

I am sure now, many years later, that she did the right thing, but for all the wrong reasons.

After the police were in the house for about ten minutes, Mary Alice drove up in her car, and, feigning surprise, came running inside.

"Oh, Dorothy, oh Dorothy," she said repeatedly, wringing her hands. "Who? Who?" she kept repeating.

Not a very good actress. She was so bad, in fact, that the RCMP had to turn their backs; even they could not condone her betraying her own daughter.

"Watch your head," said the Constable who ushered me outside and into the backseat of the car. He got in after me.

"You're quite a catch," he said.

"Am I?"

"Oh yes," he said. "And with a reward and everything to boot."

He took out his cuffs and started to place them on my wrists.

"Do you really have to do that?"

"Procedure."

"Ah, come on. I'm just a kid. I didn't kill anyone or anything," and I smiled. "Look, where am I going to go?"

He could see my logic. Even way back then, I had it, whatever *it* was.

"Well, maybe I can make an exception in your case. But don't try anything funny."

I had to admit there was some humor in the situation. It was Mary Alice who was the evil one, not me. She was free and I was going back to prison.

The article about my capture was one paragraph shorter than the one about the escape. I guess the escape was more dramatic.

Young Girl Fugitive Captured

A seventeen-year-old girl who fooled prison guards and escaped July 26, failed to fool RCMP officers in southern Alberta. Dorothy Elizabeth Mills, of Dominion, Nova Scotia, was arrested about 1:00 A.M. today by the RCMP at East Coulee a small town 90 miles east of Calgary. The young fugitive is now in custody at Calgary, awaiting transfer back to the Kingston Penitentiary where she was serving three years for robbery and auto theft.

The girl fooled her guards by stuffing two pillows under her bed covers to shape a body and then lowered herself over a prison wall with a blanket. Her escape was the first in the history of Canada's federal prison for women.

When I arrived back at Kingston, it was to a heroine's welcome.

"Hey Dorothy, led the 'Horse' on a chase, didja?"

"You sure showed 'em Dorothy."

"Attaway, Little Gangster."

"We're with you Dorothy."

This time, the gauntlet that I passed through as the guards led me back through the corridors to my cell was all congratulatory. I was a hero. For the first time in my life, I was being appreciated for my independence and my ability to survive. It was a heady feeling, almost addictive.

I continued to get attention even as the weeks passed after my return. No one was even mad at me. Even the guards were walking around shaking their heads and smiling. However, I was hauled back into court and the state asked me to pay the piper for my actions. The newspapers reported the story:

Girl Fugitive Gets Additional Six-Month Term

KINGSTON, Ont. (CP) - Dorothy Mills, seventeen, who escaped fromthe women's penitentiary here three months ago, was sentenced today to an additional six months. She will have the term added to her original sentence for armed robbery. She has served seven months of that sentence.

Magistrate J.B. Garvin, in passing sentence, said he was taking into consideration the girl's age and her "particular problems and difficulties." L.H. Pepper, the girl's lawyer, said temptation was put in the prisoner's way by a laxity of maximum security at the penitentiary.

The girl escaped July 25 after she left a dummy in her bed and climbed through a window on sheets tied together.

She later was turned over to police when she turned up in East Coulee, Alta. to visit her mother. She was the first woman to escape from a Canadian penitentiary.

To me, the prison time tacked onto my sentence made no difference. I had done the impossible. What I had proven to myself was I could formulate a plan, execute it flawlessly and bring that plan to a successful conclusion all by myself. To receive six extra months for that was well worth it to me.

I didn't know what the word "analytical" meant then. Academic prowess had never been my strong suit. But I now know and believe that I have a strong analytical mind and it was proven to me by my unorthodox actions. The first escape was necessary; the second one was pure ego.

A new prisoner named Joseline from Vancouver was put in a cell near me. People from the East or West I talked to a lot. Like me, they were ocean people. To me, they had more life in them than the landlocked folks.

Joseline and I would daydream out loud about walking along the beaches, waves and sand. Fresh seafood, ships and sailors from exotic places and the smell of salt water and summer romances.

I told her of meeting Tommy Johnson once, later of the group Tommy and Clyde, in Calgary when he had a band called the Calgary Sharks. I was involved with someone else, but Tommy and I were attracted to each other. Then the band moved to Vancouver in order to get more exposure, and changed their name to the Vancouver Sharks. They struggled, trying to break into mainstream music.

When we could raise enough money, we drank beer and smoked pot. I remember Tommy and I sleeping on the beach in each others arms. I followed him from gig to gig for awhile, but our romance ended as abruptly as it had started. I wound up involved with Emilio, the band's Gypsy guitar player.

No one got pissed off in those days. We were free spirits. I never saw Tommy again. I moved on. The next thing I knew, he was in California becoming famous. I was very happy for him. I never tried to look him up, but I did want to see him again.

Tommy represented freedom to me. California here I come. I was not going to California to try to be with Tommy romantically. That was long over. But I knew unless he had changed, he'd surely help me out.

When Joseline heard my story, she was captivated. We started to plan our getaway. Escaping to California was our dream.

First mistake—never take anyone with you. Babysitting other people slows you down. It's much easier reaching goals alone. A little help here and there, but do the work, carry the ball, all by yourself. When you're worried about the other person, you begin to be distracted. Are they going to pick up on what you're trying to do and will they go along? Also, when something goes wrong, guess who they blame?

Unfortunately, Joseline wanted to come with me so badly, I was afraid to leave her behind. I knew she could get mad at me and rat.

For the escape, I used the same method as before, only this time, we found a real ladder. They were building a new wing in the prison and all the construction equipment was supposed to be locked up at night. The ladders were not. I guess they were too big to carry. They were huge, but two women could move one to the wall. We did.

One summer night, over we went. We used the same spot was as I had the first time. I wanted to cross into New York quickly, so we crossed at "the Thousand Islands." Soon, we'd hitched a ride with a salesman named Willie on his way home to New York City. I had told Joseline what to say.

"My cousin and I are going to visit relatives in Syracuse," Joseline lied.

Willie was busy looking at my breasts, which were pulling at the buttons of my blouse. I took a deep breath to make them look even larger.

"That's right," I continued. "We're sort of shy. We'd appreciate it if you'd do the talking."

If a driver is willing to take you across a border, you know he is not too concerned with the law. And he believed our cock-and-bull story.

"No problem," Willie said, continuing to stare.

We got to Utica, New York. If I were alone, I would have spent the day there in one of the public parks, talking to people, getting the lay of the land. Maybe meeting someone who was driving to the next town. I would have continued using that strategy until there was enough distance between Kingston Prison and me. When I was halfway across the country, I would start taking rigs all the way to California.

My friend, however, wanted to start hitching right away—in broad daylight. I couldn't talk her out of it and for one of the few times in my life, I went against my better judgment. We went about hitching, and just as I was about to breath a sigh of relief, a New York State Trooper drove past, turned around and stopped. Joseline panicked and because of the state she was in, I was not able to talk us out of this one.

Back to Kingston Prison. And the wrath of the warden.

"Why did you take her with you? She was on short time. She wouldn't have done anything like that if it wasn't for you!"

Back in court, the judge gave me another six months, and I made up my mind to do my time and get the hell out of there.

What did I learn in prison?

How to be a smarter crook. How to refine what I already knew.

I got to know who was big and who was not. I could pick out which cops would cut me some slack for a blowjob from coast to coast.

Most of all, I learned I was ready for a life of crime in New York City.

CHAPTER SIX

The Dance with Demons

Heroin. In the surrealistic climate of the New York streets—drug dealers on one corner, preachers on the other—heroin was sold like there was no tomorrow. In my desperation to make it in the "big time," I would soon be sucked right into the colorful desperation, as into the vortex of a sinking ship.

Numbers runners hustled by hookers on the street, their gaudy bodies and dress enticing the cocks out of men's pants and money out of their wallets. In the doorways and halls of turn-of-the century tenements and cold water flats, junkies made themselves at home in makeshift shooting galleries, tying neckties around their veins, pumping their fists for the veins to pop up, heating smack in little spoons, drawing the liquid into syringes and, finally, injecting the deadly golden poison into their veins. With a warm rush they'd settle back for the high of their life.

In the glare of the midday sun back out on the street, every kind of snake oil salesman known to man was hustling. Hustling, hustling, hustling.

And how else could all these criminal enterprises function unless it was sanctioned from on high? There were load upon load of cops on the take, from the lowest patrolmen right on up through the ranks. It seemed that everyone was on the pad. Everyone.

Mixed in with the sounds of police sirens were people screaming and laughing, children bawling and the squall of music, lots of music. It dominated the street and came from every window, newsstand, restaurant and bar. Jazz, blues and salsa surrounded me like a sonic umbrella as I walked up and down the street.

My reports said every group had a few blocks that unofficially belonged to the head man of the time. I had to decide which group I was going to belong to. East Side, West Side, White, Black. From my purse I took a coin and flipped it. Harlem won. My name would be "Chickie" again.

When I arrived in New York, I was poor—no money, one change of clothes and most importantly, no class.

How did I get to the Big Apple without money? Simple. My old standby. Eighteen wheeler from Montreal to New York. Then it was simple. Hail a taxi and take it from there down to Harlem on the other side of the East River. Only problem was, it was night.

"Where ya goin' lady?"

The taxi driver leaned out of his car and looked me over.

"Harlem."

He shook his head. "No way. Not at this time a night."

"Look," I said, leaning in closer and resting my hands on the downturned window. "I really would be most appreciative if you could take me. See, I'm new . . ."

And as I continued to give him this cock-and-bull story, I lowered my voice to its most seductive level and arched my shoulders so my breasts shot out, high and proud, until he had a good view of my top 40.

"Sure," he finally relented, not taking his eyes off my nipples poking through the fabric of my thin shirt. "Hop in."

And off we went, down Broadway. I looked out as the greatest city in the world passed by my speeding window. I couldn't help but smile. I knew I'd do well here.

When we got to Harlem, I looked for a good place to stop where I could run for it. I didn't have enough money to pay cab fare. Then I saw it, a bar, with an entrance right on the corner. That meant there'd be a sidedoor on the side street, and I could hide in a stairwell or doorway until the driver got frustrated and drove away. Cool. I knew that he would not hang around Harlem long.

At the light, I bolted out of the cab and made a run for it.

"Hey! Where the fuck—"

I never heard the rest of what he said, because I was through the door of the bar in an instant. What I saw stopped me in my tracks.

The bar was dimly lit with a shock of light coming from the cigarette machine and the jukebox. Some street lights flashed their night message and the neon reflected on the bar's window and the cash register. Smoke from cigarettes and cigars rose dreamily through the shafts of lights.

The patrons were all black. Some had skin the color of copper, others like topaz or onyx that shone as the light hit them.

I was stunned and rooted to the spot. I understood for the first time why White America was afraid of blacks. When these people became empowered with the knowledge of who they really were, they would be a force to be reckoned with.

The prison grapevine had let me know who were the top dealers in every area.

In Harlem, Raymond Marquize seemed to be the man of power at that time. Richard Hill, "Big" Jimmie Bell and "Cadillac" Richard Wheeler were also vying for their place in the sun of the criminal aboveground. Richie Wheeler in particular was moving up fast as one of the top heroin dealers on the East Coast.

"Cadillac" Richie, so named for his favorite mode of transportation, was fearless. Hill was like a dog with a bone, so persistent that only a bullet in the brain would stop him. Bell was not a threat to either man because he was not in the drug game.

Big Jimmie's thing was bookmaking. He'd take bets on any-thing—baseball, football, basketball, hockey, whatever the sport of the season was. He also ran numbers—you pick the number of the winning horses at the local racetracks—backroom poker and craps games. He controlled a large area and he made big money, but he refused to cross over into the drug trade. So the only thing the boys had to fear was that he would never cover for them if it came to that.at.

There were other bigger players moving around Harlem than the ones I already mentioned. Sam Hawkins, Frank Mathews, all of them belonging to a sub-culture that was so ostentatious and opulent, it blinded me to the suffering and despair of the people around me. The players were feeding off the people like sharks in an aquarium.

I was a very young woman, all I wanted was the beautiful clothes, the silkiest furs, the most elegant jewelry and the longest cars. Once and for all, I would not want for anything. Once and for all, people would look up to me. Once and for all I would be the one who didn't get the sharp end of the stick. I'd be the one feared and respected. I'd be the rich one.

I stared at the bar's patrons wide-eyed.

"What the fuck you lookin' at? Is you or ain't you a nigger, honey?"

"Who cares? Hey, I saw her first. Gimme a piece a dat ass!"

I couldn't believe it. I blinked. These kings and queens speak-ing like, like . . .

"Man, get the fuck outta my face. Dat little yella gal don't want you."

"Who says?" White teeth flashed in a big black face. "Come on over here, sugar. Big Daddy'll look after ya."

Another one laughed. "Shit, nigger! That bitch so full of juice, she just about drown ya."

"You can't handle that," a beautiful, onyx-skinned lady said. "Why don't you all shut the fuck up—"

"Ooh, Ooh," the men chimed in unison.

". . . and see what the girl want. Honey, what can we do for ya?"

"Well please, m'am, I'd like to leave by the side door. See there's a white man outside I'm trying to avoid. I owe him some money I don't have," I said in the most plaintive voice I could muster.

No one knew me. No one cared about the debt I owed for the cab ride. Given the tenor of the times, any suggestion of impropriety towards a black or near a black was reason to riot. Quickly, I was ushered to the side door exit. Out I went to the cheers of the living wall of black men and women.

Outside, the night air was warm and the smells that only humans create, wafted up and permeated my nostrils. It was the smell of life and suddenly, my step was buoyant.

The side street was 116th Street. Lights were on all over the place, a very rare thing in the ghettos I had seen before. The block was busy, busy with people hanging in stairwells, waiting, always waiting.

Kids played stoop ball, throwing pink Spaldings against stoops and trying to catch them on the fly.

Mothers sat on stoops with new babies, trying to get some air because their apartments were too hot.

As I walked down the street, I could hear a ballgame coming from numerous radios, an echo all the way down the block. It was the Yankees, the world famous Bronx Bombers.

"Score's two to two, tied in the seventh. Batter up. He swings—a Ballantine blast!" shouted Mel Allen, the announcer.

Winos crowded around wastebaskets drinking their life-giving fuel, wines with names like Slick, Patches, Big Moe and Ninety-Nine. Drinking out of the bottle openly was a violation of state law; crumpled paper sacks were the preferred means of disguising the brew, but one look at their bloodshot eyes and rumpled appearance gave a signal as to what they drank and what they really were.

In a slow wave, it was all coming at me. My eyes, ears, all my senses strained to take the stimuli in, to make sense of it, to shift it, to figure out the lay of the land and how I was going to survive here.

A big, white Lincoln Continental with fins that looked as razor sharp as a shark's, glided down the street and stopped in front of a building. Doors opened and finely dressed black men and women emerged and stood receiving compliments from the peons that crowded around them. A nod here, a wink there, handshakes all around.

Suddenly, I realized that I had accidentally stumbled onto a stage, an elaborate set of props, lights, actors and actresses. The camera was my eyes. As I was recording the images in the dark room of my mind, to be taken out and studied later for what I could learn and use, the lens of the camera began to open wider.

Two very shabbily dressed young men approached the group of beautiful people. A dirty hand touched the sleeve of the suit jacket that one of the men was so graciously modeling for the audience that had gathered. The gentleman's reactions were swift and savage.

Fists sprang out quicker than the eye could follow, pummeling the dirty young vagabond. Legs came up in kicks that landed with savage grace in loud, muffled thuds that made your face scrunch up and wince in sympathetic pain. As the shabby man fell, his tormentor continued to kick him.

"Come on, I didn't mean nothing', please don't—" the shabby man shouted. The "gentleman" continued to beat him senseless.

"Please, stop, we just wanted to score," the shabby man's friend shouted. "He's sick sir, we'll do anything Big Man, just say so."

The fashionable man breathed harder, in and out, exhausted by the beating he had given the man who was a bloody mess, twisted into a fetal position on the ground.

"Please, no more," his friend begged.

Spit ran down the friend's chin as, wild-eyed with terror, he looked around for help. A crowd with many able-bodied people had gathered to watch the beating, but not one person stepped forward.

"Please Big Man, I'll do whatever you say for a fix," the friend begged.

With that, Big Man's fist shot out and hit the fellow so hard, he crumpled to the ground next to his friend. Then a lady who was part of the well-dressed party became so impatient, she stomped her high-heeled foot.

"Daddy, stop that right now!"

Big Man angrily looked down at the two people writhing on the ground, but he kept his fists at his side and his feet close together.

"Look at y'all," his lady friend continued, "y'all getting all mussed up. Looka that. Don't get blood all over your clothes. Now you'll have to wash up at the party. You ain't gonna touch me after having your hands all over that junkie."

That scored. Keep hitting, no titty. Big Man backed off. Taking out a huge roll of bills, Big Man passed out twenties to some of the people gathered.

"Go'bout ya'all's business now, it's over. Go on home now," shouted Big Man. Mothers with babies, winos, young children as well as old men and women crowded in to get some of the free money. Some weren't impressed. They stood back watching.

"Man, I'm angry at dat man," said one woman.

"Black devils, living high off the hog," declared a second.

"Selling drugs to they own kind," an older man chimed in.

"Passin' money around as if some small kindness will excuse them for destroying they own people," the first woman proclaimed.

"Them poor junkies they beat up paid for that car and them clothes. Put that bank roll in their pockets. Now they come back to the neighborhood beating up them poor junkies," the second woman chimed in with her two cents.

Another woman nearby told everyone within earshot, "The mighty shall fall."

"That's right," said the first man. "Look at those young girls."

"Should be in school," the second man added.

"Whores of Babylon!"

"Breaking their poor mommas hearts."

As if they had heard or didn't care, the fancy ladies beamed as they took hold of their men's arms and sashayed into the building where the party was.

"When those men are finished wit 'em, they'll come out looking like a well-traveled road," the first lady said grimly.

As I watched, the crowd on 116th Street on that hot summer's night, my first night in Harlem, my thoughts turned to a more pressing matter—my own survival.

I was hungry. I was dirty and needed a bath. I didn't have a place to sleep.

I knew that I couldn't fit in until I learned the language. The people were speaking in Black American English. What did I know of that? I knew that I would have to test some of my repertoire of characters to figure out what worked with these people.

Would I act docile and helpless? No, that wouldn't work. Everyone around here respected strength. Acting weak would only make me a target, something I vowed I would not be any more.

So I decided on strong and confident. If I wanted Mr. Big and his buddies to notice me, I would have to be hard to get.

Innately, I understood that bad guys loved class. A woman with real class did two things for a lowlife. It made them look good and they could learn social graciousness. Most of them still farted in public.

I would make them see that I was an asset. Admittedly, that would take some time, and while I was doing that, there was the little matter of my day-to-day survival to take care of.

A temporary method, one I'd used in the past, was to use the dynamic of human nature. People are willing to help you if you show a desire to help yourself. So I walked along Eighth Avenue and went into every bar and offered my services as a dishwasher, general clean-up person or waitress.

"I'm also looking for room and board but I need some hard cash right away," I would add.

I knew the approach would work. After just a few days of canvasing, I found menial labor and a room above one of the bars. They gave me a few dollars in advance.

The first thing I did with my money was to buy some clothes to wear that would draw attention to my well built, youthful body. I also reported to work an hour early, and worked very hard. That was more for my sake than my employer's. It gave me a whole hour to network with the patrons, to talk, to look, to listen.

In the ghetto, people don't ask questions of other people. As long as you keep your place, stay out of the way and don't repeat what you hear or see, everything will be okay.

I also didn't show any fear. I walked around Harlem all day and night, taking it all in, like an actor learning the background of a play he was acting in.

Harlem was a feast of contradictions. Despair existed side by side with hope. Pockets of poverty comparable only to the black hole of Calcutta, mixed in with excessive spending on the part of some of the neighborhood's wealthier inhabitants. And stunning beauty stood next to gnarled, life-beaten bodies too stubborn to die.

Junkies stayed in the shadows, waiting to pounce. It amazed me to see how they would start to gather like vultures several times a day to score their dope.

Every group had a connection. I watched them as they jockeyed for position to be first when the street dealer showed on time, always on time. Their inner clocks were synchronized to the call of the Beast.

At every meeting, there would inevitably be a small conflict. A junkie would come up short or he wouldn't have the money to cover a previous buy. A short-lived drama began—some begging, crying and threatening and finally, a meeting of minds.

After the act was over, the junkies scurried like rats back to their holes to shoot up. The street pusher returned to his connection with the money and re-upped for the next act of the dance with demons.

I stood by, curious, witnessing the play. I didn't yet have an understanding of what I was witnessing, let alone know that sometime in the near future I would be living large off these poor, twisted souls.

As the days passed, I got comfortable with my environment and became part of a group of made-up, colorful characters: young "wannabes" waiting for the big break, some of them actually making it happen. I couldn't be as bold as they were because I didn't want to get caught. I was an illegal, and I had a long way to go before I looked, acted and talked like a local.

Despite my usual flair, the language was a bitch to master. It was the way words were linked together, code talk that differed depending on where the speakers came from. And all that jargon was mixed in with northern street slang, street colloquialisms and schooling, if there was any. To be totally accepted, I had to become literate in it.

I studied and studied and after awhile, I began to speak the lingo. As my confidence grew, I started to relax. I let it be known among my street group that I was ambitious.

"Looking to make some big money, huh Chickie?"

"That's right. You got it."

I knew that I had to somehow let the big players know that I was for hire. By now, I had met many of them—Mellow, Freako, Zack, Raymond, Rock, Moon, Scottie, Ralph, Vince, Daddy, Goldfinger, Sweets, and many more. All of them were major players in the dope racket. I didn't have the guts to ask them for work. In the meantime, I just hung around the bars, trying to catch a play.

I wasn't sleeping with any of these guys. Hell, I couldn't get close enough to start anything with them. They never came in the bars alone. Always, they had an entourage of partners, bodyguards and beautiful women.

I played the waiting game, but after awhile, I felt that I was losing. I wasn't going to break through to the higher echelon. Maybe I should go back to Montreal. I could always make a big score there where I knew the territory and the players and the action like the back of my hand, and return to New York with my own money.

What I needed was the appearance of good luck and prosperity. That was something taught to me in prison.

"Remember kid," one of the older inmates told me, "if you want to impress someone, you gotta act like you're just as flush as they are."

This advice wasn't any different than for someone working in the legitimate sector. If you looked rich and prosperous, and you acted confident and not desperate, you'd attract a like kind.

I never stayed any place more than three to four months because I got bored very easily, so I really wasn't upset by the prospect of leaving Harlem, but I didn't want to leave a failure. All the people I knew who had come to New York and returned for a visit, came back with pockets full of money, designer clothes, jewelry and big, flashy, new cars.

Sitting on a bar stool in a two-for-one joint on the corner of 110th Street and Eight Avenue, I was working all of this out in my head. Only the brave or the crazy—I belong to the latter category—hung out at that corner, where Spanish Harlem and Black Harlem crashed into each other, not unlike a head-on collision between two locomotives with full loads.

God I loved that corner. For hours, I would sit by the window and watch all the actions of the people passing by—the changing body language of the men and women crossing 110th Street. I loved two-for-ones. It felt like you're getting something for nothing.

"Hispanic," I murmured. I watched them intently and filed still another role in my head for another day.

The Spanish junkies would hesitate to move more than one block up Eighth Avenue to meet their connection; and, in the event of a conflict between junkie and pusher, the pusher would not give chase across 110th Street. Everyone was on high alert.

In addition to their liberal drinking policy, the bar I hung out in was a meeting place for Latinos and African Americans who came together in order to work out details of a big drug shipment and tell each other how, if they worked together, everybody would get rich.

Sometimes, one of the Latino drug honchos would try to make time with me.

"¿ Que pasa, senorita?"

I had made a slight change in my makeup and hair again, and so could now pass as a Latina. I had also picked up a few words and phrases in Spanish, but it would be a while before I became fluent in the Latinos' form of ghetto talk.

After a couple minutes of his questions, I'd usually say, "No hablo español, Pac." All my buddies in the bar would laugh, while the Latino, his macho ego in tatters, would slink away. I was struggling with too many identities at this time to make them all work perfectly, but I could deliver a put-down in any language.

Guys like that distracted me from my serious thoughts until one day, in walked a young man, about twenty-seven-years-old. He walked with the fluidity of a fine dancer. I couldn't take my eyes off of him. In the ghetto, it was considered dangerous to stare. Still, I couldn't help it. Besides, I wasn't staring at the dude because he was the most handsome specimen of human male flesh I had ever seen.

I stared at him because I knew him. But for the life of me, I couldn't figure out from where.

He stared back at me.

"Hey Babe, don't I know you from someplace?"

That sure punctured the balloon. When he caught himself, even he had to smile.

"Did I say that?"

That broke the ice.

"Yes, you did," I laughed.

"Hey, how 'bout a round of drinks?" he said to the bartender.

There were twenty people in the joint, and he was running the bar. Either he had money or he was a good actor.

"Hi, my name is Richard Wheeler," he said suavely.

"Hi, my name is Chickie."

He had not gotten his nickname yet, "Cadillac Richie." In the not too distant future, he would be a powerful gangster. But then, he was still on his way up.

As we talked we began to seriously explore where we knew each other from.

"It's not New York," said Richard.

"No, not New York," I agreed.

"And you're from Montreal?"

"Mmm-hmm," I sipped my drink and studied his face, trying to place him.

"Well, I been to Canada, but not—"

"Vancouver!" I shouted.

"How'd you know . . . wait a second. When I was in the Army, I was stationed across the border in Seattle."

"And you used to come to Vancouver on leave and visit your girlfriend who was—"

"A hooker. Right. I was with her for awhile. We had a real good time together."

"I remember," I said.

Richard Wheeler may not yet have arrived on the Harlem drug scene, but he was making his presence known. At this point he was a stick-up man and had come to the corner bar to meet a guy and discuss a "score."

"What are you doing around here?" he asked me.

When I filled him in on my situation, he offered me some work.

I wasn't afraid of heists or hold-ups, armed or otherwise. I had been part of many in Montreal, which is known throughout the provinces as the heist capital of Canada. But working with Richard, I would have the added protection of guaranteed bail if we got caught, and of course, I could jump bail and get back across the border to Canada if I was caught.

The next day, Richard got me an ID, so that the authorities would think I was an American. He presented me with my very own New Jersey birth certificate and driver's license. "Aloma Johnson, Camden, New Jersey," it read.

I didn't even have to take the road test.

My first hold-up with Richard involved a big-time drug dealer.

"You're going to be the decoy," Richard explained. "I've studied the guy's movements for months. We're going to take him down."

Richard thrust a gun into my palm and we got into a stolen vehicle. The driver had stolen a bright red car that kept stalling. Then we got lost in the Bronx. As we bumped around the streets, one of the guns with a hair trigger went off.

"Son-of-a-bitch!" I yelled.

"Cock sucker, you almost took my head off!" Richard added.

After more swearing and threats, we settled down and found the address. It turned out that we'd passed the building several times.

The driver parked a block away. He was supposed to leave the car running, while Richard and I went inside. My job was to get on the intercom and lure the target out of his apartment, down to the lobby of his building. Then Richard would ambush him and take him by gunpoint back to his apartment, tie him up, take all the money and drugs, and we'd make our getaway.

Well, sure, that sounds great. But to make it happen was going to be a test of our larcenist minds.

The first part was easy. The target answered my ring in a cautious, tough voice.

"Yeah, who is it?"

"It's Sally."

"I don't know any Sally. Who—"

"Don't you remember? We met at Jonesy's Place. You told me if I was ever up in your neighborhood to look you up. Well, here I am."

There was a pause. "Jonesy's Place? When?"

"Last week," I lied.

"Describe yourself."

There I was, talking into an inanimate piece of metal covered with graffiti and trying to make my voice sexy.

"Well," I purred into the intercom, "I'm sort of tall, especially in the heels I have on now, I have black hair, and I'm sort of, well, you know, voluptuous. When we met, you liked the dress I was wearing. You said it looked like I'd been poured into it."

Another pause.

The idea was to seduce the drug dealer from his den, to make him feel comfortable and take him off his guard. When he came to the door, he wouldn't be able to slam it in my face if, in fact, he opened it to see me in my tight leather dress and spiked high heels. And Richard, who would be standing next to me, would take care of the rest.

"I'm coming down," the man said over the intercom and buzzed. "Wait in the lobby."

So much for well-laid plans. Richard brushed by me and disappeared into the dark interior.

A minute later, the door to the stairwell opened and a man came out. He was halfway across the lobby before he realized he didn't know me.

"Say, what—"

Richard came up behind him, and stuck the gun in the man's ear just as the target swung around, pulling his own gun out of his pants. That was something we hadn't counted on.

Their guns up in the air, Richard and the man struggled, trying to get into position to fire. I couldn't shoot, because they were too close together. I might miss and hit Richard. I couldn't speak or act but I was acutely aware of everything happening.

I was aware of how the very bright and hot sun had not been strong enough to overpower the darkness of the cold marble, cast iron metal and wood interior.

I was aware of the smell of disinfectant from a thousand scrubbings permeating the lobby.

I was aware of the building's once grand, neoclassical architecture that stubbornly clung to its grand facade deep inside a rapidly decaying neighborhood.

I was aware of children's laughter and mothers' scoldings.

I was aware of all of this as God reached out his hand and gently saved my worthless life by deflecting an oncoming bullet that only grazed the right side of my head, leaving a part where the hair had been scorched off.

With that gunshot, everyone panicked. Richard and I lost control. The only thing to do was run. My ability to move instantaneously returned. We hit the street at a fast trot and ran to our getaway car. We could hear the motor trying to turn over. Behind us, the drug dealer was in hot pursuit.

We jumped into the car and as the motor coughed to life. The car moved very slowly away from the curb and into traffic. We put a block between us and the dealer, who by that time had been joined by a few of his buddies. Then the motor coughed one last time and died.

Opening the car doors, we made a mad dash onto the street and raced across the avenue. Everyone took a different route back to Harlem. The driver hot-wired a car. I grabbed a cab and Richard took a bus.

It was a good thing there was no such thing as "exact fare" at that time. Otherwise, that would have been the end of Cadillac Richie's career.

Back at the Sky Club on Eighth and 112th, we all met over drinks and laughed so hard we cried. Richard told the story of our adventure to anyone who was around, whether they wanted to hear or not. As we continued to laugh, I realized that for the first time in my deadly serious life, I had learned how to laugh at myself.

CHAPTER SEVEN

The Shooter

After that episode, Richie and I partnered on about eight to ten stick-ups. Unlike the first, where we were closer to "the gang that couldn't shoot straight," these were all successful. Even though in the eyes of the law we were guilty of armed robbery each time we robbed someone, my conscience had an easier time because all the targets were bad guys. My reputation grew.

"She's a solid broad."

"Solid, man, solid."

"Chickie's got a solid rep, man."

Solid, solid, solid. That's how I was described and how I began to be perceived in all the bars and clubs we frequented. To my pleasure, I got the respect that was normally due a gangster with balls.

While I was in the hold-up business with Richard Wheeler, I met a dealer from "Little Italy," Leo Valenti. Between jobs, I worked for him in his heroin processing factories. I quickly found out Leo didn't pay his workers very well. Still, I needed the extra bread because the hold-ups Cadillac Richie and I did never brought us more than thirty thousand. By the time we paid the driver and split the rest, it didn't make us rich. And I spent money as fast as I made it. It's easy in the fast lane to spend thousands a day. I needed more. That's how I came to work in my first heroin factory.

It was one of many run by Leo, so influential and so powerful; it was said he had many high-ranking officials in New York City in his hip pocket.

I always knew when a shipment of dope came in for Leo because the runners, bodyguards, seconds-in-command, everyone would be in and out of the bars all up and down the street, looking.

"Looking for what?" I asked Cadillac Richie, before I knew about such things.

"They're lookin' for workers, Chickie. Women to work in the heroin factories."

All the women they could round up went to work. Wives, girlfriends, friends, sisters, even some of the mothers of the Mob members. When there weren't enough from these ranks, the pick-ups started. Word went out and any woman interested should be at a certain bar at a certain time the next day. This message was delivered all over. Depending on the size of the shipment, different bars and times would be used for different neighborhoods.

It was like a cattle call for the theater, but this was really theater of the absurd. The women who answered the call were poor, often had kids, and were living on the edge trying to make a few extra dollars. They'd do anything to make their squalid lives easier. They never thought that those same drugs they processed for sale eventually wound up in their children's veins.

This was one way the dealers had to keep the common folks behind them. They knew that they could buy the loyalty of the poor people by giving them a chance to make a few dollars, and the biggest employer at that time was Leo Valenti.

"How can I get a factory job?" I asked Wheeler.

"I know some of the players," Richie replied. "When one of 'em comes into the bar, I'll put a bug in his ear."

And just like that, I was hired.

Four of us, Dayna, Iris, Rolanda and I were sitting at the Bigtime Bar the next day when the driver picked us up in a white Chevy Impala.

"Hi, I'm Ross," said the driver. "Let's go ladies. Ya'll want to make some money, right?"

We all muttered our assent and piled into the Impala. During the ride, we didn't talk much. I only knew Rolanda. She was a bar fly at a nearby place where I hung out. The others I'd seen around.

Ross stopped a few times to make phone calls and even took us to a bar for drinks. Once we arrived at our destination, though, he got very cautious and tooled around for an hour before pulling up in front of a dismal gray brownstone apartment building. I noticed spotters on the stoop. They disappeared quickly.

"Come on ladies, let's go," and Ross hustled us inside.

We followed him up two flights of rickety stairs into a small, sparsely furnished apartment. All the windows were blacked out with blinds and blankets. There was a strong smell of chemicals in the air. The mixer, a brown-skinned woman with a thin, lined face, was just finishing up her duties, leaving the table all set up for us.

The mixing table was covered with industrial plastic drawn taut and fastened under the table to keep it from moving about. Playing cards, large strainers, nylons and gauze, measuring spoons and regular kitchen table spoons and scales. That was our paraphernalia, placed neatly at each place on the table.

"In here," said one of the guards, and he led us into the bedroom. "Okay, now strip down," he ordered.

We quickly stripped to our underwear. A huge woman with a prizefighter's flattened face and cauliflower ears stepped into the room and without a word searched each of us, while a big, ugly ape of a man covered us with a .44 Magnum. The ape's look said, "You'd better not have come in with anything," meaning guns, wires or small bags to carry any dope you might steal.

"And don't even think of leaving with anything," his look said with a neanderthal-browed glower.

After they were finished with us, we watched as some other girls were brought in and put through the same drill. When we were all ready, they hustled us out of the room.

"Sit at the long table," the woman with the prizefighter's face said. I looked around.

There were two men at the door and two in the room with us. I remembered the spotters on the stoop of the building.

Several women sat at the table. One woman functioned as the spooner. In front of her, she had a pile of mixed drugs and a tipped measuring spoon, so as not to give too much to a fix. You see, the first thing to be determined was how good the smack was. How'd they know? They used a human guinea pig.

A junkie would be given a free fix and they watched to see how he responded. If he OD'd, the spoon would be tipped. Tipped means that an obstacle was put into place right at the tip of the spoon. Held there by tape, it prevented a full portion from flowing into the bag. They didn't want to fill the bag with more drug than was needed. A pile of stamp bags were beside the spooner, ready for her to fill each one with lightning speed.

To the spooner's right sat the folder. This one was hardly more than a child. She took the open bag from the spooner, shook the dope down, folded the flap over once, and folded the bag in half, then passed it to the taper.

The blond, light-skinned taper put a small amount of tape on the fold and passed it to the staker. The staker made bundles of twenty-five of these bags and put rubber bands around them and dropped the bundles into a large, brown paper bag sitting on the floor. When that bag was full, it was time for the next shift.

When our shift finished, one at a time we were escorted to the bathroom. The woman with the prizefighter's face searched inside our bras and panties, allowed us to wash up, and then hustled us back to the bedroom to get dressed. When all the crew was ready to go, we got paid by one of the guards, and Ross drove us back to the bar where we began in the white Impala.

That first day, I learned Leo was a cheapskate. For an eight hour shift, we made two-hundred dollars each. The spooner made more but not enough for all the work she did. It was the mixer who got the good money, because she was the girlfriend of the boss or second-in-command.

I worked in the factories long enough to learn the whole process. I didn't just learn how to mix, spoon, etc.; I really learned the business. I learned how to look for the apartments that could be turned into drug factories. Where on the street the building should be situated. Which floor was the best. What side of the building the apartment should be on and what street the windows should be facing. Who the neighbors were and if the super could be paid off.

My brief experience with Leo Valenti gave me another look at the business, long enough for me to know that I did not want to work with or for people like him. However, I couldn't help but notice Leo V. was taking a special interest in me, and I already knew he was one man I did not want to know better. There were loud rumors on the street that he was into sadism and I believed it. There was something very off about the man, and he was always mean when he talked to his women.

Shortly after I had sized him up, I decided I had learned enough and when the next cattle calls came, I didn't show. The next time I saw Leo was at the Metro Club, the same day that famous comedian Bill Cosby and his entourage came in and sat at a table near me. I shook his hand and was thrilled.

"Nice to see you again, Mr. Cosby."

"And nice to see you again young lady," he said.

We had met in Toronto; he spent a lot of time there, where I think he was involved in a business venture with football people. Often, we ran into each other socially. There was a men's shop on Yarbrough Street he liked to frequent, and I knew the owners.

Bill seemed to remember me, and I was pleased. But who knows? Maybe he was just being polite to a fan. Anyway, later in the evening, he was invited up to the stage and he accepted. He did a few jokes, more like funny stories about the products he endorsed on T.V. While Bill was performing, Leo Valenti strode in like he owned the place. Leo started to prance around like a stallion, talking loud and trying to get all the attention to himself. When he saw me, he came over.

"Yo, bitch! What you mean quittin' me?" he said as loud and as angrily he could.

Everyone nearby knew what he was talking about. I was embarrassed because I did not want to be singled out for unwanted attention in front of Bill Cosby's friends. Bill had treated me like a lady, and in walked Leo Valenti to ruin it for me.

When Bill was finished on stage, he came down and sat with his friends. Admirers surrounded him. I wanted to go over and compliment him, but I just couldn't. I was so ashamed. Bill thought I was a businesswoman, not some sleazy drug dealer.

Walking out, I brushed by his table.

"Hi," he called. "How're you doing?"

The famous entertainer's voice faded as I approached the street and disappeared into the late evening traffic.

After our last stick-up, things started to get too hot for Cadillac Richie and me. Friends of the people we'd held up were looking for us, not to mention the cops who were wondering who this new stick-up team was. If we were going to operate in their territory, they wanted part of our action. It was a good time for me to take a powder and visit somewhere else.

I decided on Montreal. I was lookin' real good when I got there—fine threads, a bank roll as big as a horse's balls, furs, the whole schmear, but it took less than two weeks before I was broke. I lost all the money I had by running the bars in my favorite hangouts, parties, gifts, dinners for twelve and a trip to

Toronto and back—first class. Soon, the only thing I was flush with was the wall. I had to get back to New York and the big money.

Change happens very fast on the street, in the space that it takes for an eye to be replaced by a bullet hole. When I got back to New York, Cadillac Richie had partnered with the Black Mafia. He was now into drugs in a huge way.

"Of course there's room for my old partner," he said in answer to my query.

I had no idea what the business of drugs was about. It blew my mind that a few hours work would bring such large dividends. At the Mafia level of distribution, a worker could buy a new car out of the showroom window from a day's proceeds. A week's work could buy a house.

A furrier I knew at the time, a Jewish man who lived in East Flatbush in Brooklyn, would complain to me that he worked long, hard hours and never had the type of money necessary to buy such things. He would see black men on the street driving their fancy Cadillacs, and felt rabidly angry that they could afford such things and he could not.

Of course, I know that those cars and those houses had come from drugs, gambling or pimping money. The majority of the people in the ghetto didn't have money for bus fare, let alone fancy possessions.

Despite the power of the drug organizations, there were people in the neighborhood violently against drugs. Resistance, though, was useless. Those people could not win. The army of men and women in the drug game was stronger. Not only did they have money, they knew how to use it to bribe cops and politicians, so the drug trade could flourish.

Vancouver was the drug mecca of Canada. I had seen the drug business there first-hand, but nothing prepared me for this nether world of greed and destruction. It was the fastest rising American business, more than munitions, more than real estate, more than stocks and bonds.

As I was learning the trade—pick-up, delivery, muling, stashing, weighing, mixing, collecting and negotiation—I was thrown into a world of furs, designer cars and clothes, expensive jewelry and fine wines. Lavish food cost $50 a bite, and the names of the dishes I was eating were practically unpronounceable.

Any event I wanted to attend—baseball or football games, concerts, Broadway shows, even sell-outs—was open to me because of the money I made pulling heists with Richie. We could always get tickets as gifts from either our suppliers or our heavy downtown clients.

Respectability was something I could now afford to buy, or so I thought. Having drinks with politicians, movie stars, sports celebrities, bankers, even judges, made me feel very special. It never dawned on me that these people hid under a veneer of respectability made from a combination of looks, money and power. All I saw was the surface. If I had bothered to think, I would have realized that they were not respectable simply because they were associating with dealers like us. These people were so stupid and full of themselves, so much into debauchery and hedonism, it never occurred to them that eventually, we would be the ones responsible for pouring the poison into their own children's veins.

Yes, we were celebrities in the drug world. But when push came to shove, we were still heroin dealers. We were experts at using intimidation to keep the very people in line who we were killing and destroying. Did I notice the runny noses, the vacant eyes, the scratching and twitching, the ash that would form on the corner of the mouth from dried drool, and the awful smell that comes off a sick junkie?

Yes, I did, and I was one of the many "doctors" that could provide temporary relief for a very large fee.

To get away from such misery was easy. Those images would soon fade over a bottle of Moet and Chandon champagne, with

Beluga caviar and Oysters Rockefeller. Yet I had begun to question the sense of this fast lane, jet set lifestyle. How much expensive food could you eat before it gave you the runs? How many drinks could you ingest before the hangovers became too much and your liver became damaged? How many people could you meet whose names you soon forgot? How much money could you spend in a day before you were broke? How many countries could you travel to just in order to go shopping? And how much loneliness could you really tolerate?

I had no sense of accomplishment, only a bitter taste in my mouth at the end of a day. Days and nights became one. Relationships that were forged in the twin crucibles of greed and death ignited then burned out. Just wrecked ships passing in the night and then floundering on the rock of reality.

Sex . . . sex was casual. Often times, women and men in the business would cement a deal with a night of lustful intoxication. But we didn't sell ourselves short or for cheap. For this Bacchus-like behavior to take place, at least a million dollars in a drug deal had to be at stake.

And so it went for five years as I languished in the drug trade.

From time to time, I made trips to Canada, just to rest. These visits would only last a few weeks, because I soon found that I had outgrown most of my old friends. They were still pimping and whoring and committing petty crimes. I made a big show of my power and money. Even their adoration didn't sustain me, though.

Enter—cocaine.

The code of the big-time players was "NO DRUGS."

"Hey, I won't do business with you. You're smoking a joint," I remember saying to one of my drug dealer contacts.

The word was that drugs made one careless, lazy, stupid and dangerous to the organization. After third man up—first man, street junkie, second man, his connection (the runner) and third man, the supplier—drug use was not acceptable. When it came to the distributors, brokers, bankers,factory workers, mules, etc., drugs were out.

A person who was a junkie only knew his or her street connection. The street connection would only know one to three street suppliers. The street suppliers would pick up from a representative of a distributor. By maintaining this level of security, the people above the level of distributor, the real money people, would always be protected.

I knew the rules and played by them. I was in big demand because of my talents. Being a free agent, I could work for the highest bidder—and did.

Still, I was an empty shell, tired and weak. I was in total darkness. All my actions had grown mechanical. I operated without spirit, soul or conscience as a representative of a drug distributor. Depressed and unhappy, I gradually started to do a few lines of cocaine with Cadillac Richie, who had finally achieved enough success to merit his nickname. To my surprise, I found out many of our associates were also into the bag.

Richie told me, "It gives you more energy when you have to work around the clock in the factories, and it will spice up your sex life, and it's not habit forming, and . . ." Lies. All lies.

Cocaine is the biggest deceiver of all drugs. It causes strong, psychological dependence. It's possibleto die from a small dose. Paranoid psychosis, anxiety, serious damage to the nervous system, on and on go the results of addiction. But when people first start taking coke, they believe they have discovered gold. Heaven on earth—euphoria, exhilaration!

The drug attacks part of the brain in healthy people. Suddenly, judgment calls falter, clear-headed decision making is more difficult, and in the world of gangsterdom, being alert at all times is a tremendous asset.

After a while, cocaine makes the difficult impossible. It becomes your boss. It did that to me. I started to go to bed with men that I wouldn't shake hands with under normal circumstances. I would stay in bed for days at a time, eating solid food only about three times a week, and drinking rye, cognac, gin and rum all day, everyday. I lost weight. My clothes didn't fit. Underneath my eyes were deep circles.

There is a class heirarchy in the underworld, and I was sliding down the ladder. The money was still there, I could still hide my problem from the main guys, but slowly I started to make mistakes. Not being on time, talking out of turn, being short on some cash, not being available for weeks at a time and the worst— bringing people with me to a meeting who were not part of the organization, thereby compromising everyone's security.

Cocaine has the ability to take the most docile characters and turn them into raging bulls. I was confused, unstable, immature and out of control. The more that stuff went up my nose, the worse my attitude got. In public, I was loud and rude. My new "friends," my fellow users, were as messed up as I was. We'd take over bars and restaurants with our bold, aggressive stance. The high rollers began backing away from me. The word went out.

"Chickie has a 'Coke Jones.' She can't take care of business."

Occaisirislly, I'd try to stop, though not long enough to make a difference, and very soon I'd be back to the bag. It was during this time that I met the most unusual man I'd ever known.

His street image was striking. He was called "the Black Prince," and black he was, jet black like onyx. Not too tall, about 5'8", one hundred pounds, hair cut very close to his head, small, neat feet that made him walk with a mincing gate. He had a very shrill laugh, like a woman's. Unlike the apartment in which he lived, he was very meticulous about his appearance. Of course, he looked old to me. When you're young, anyone five years older looks ancient.

He lived in a roach-infested ghetto apartment in Harlem. Dirt, garbage and clothes were strewn all over. It was a one bedroom flat, with one bathroom, a kitchen and a living room. Old, broken-down furniture. Everything was old except his wardrobe and jewelry.

His name was Richard Hill, and he was about forty-years-old when I first saw him standing at the bar in a hot new Harlem nightclub. He always wore a fedora, breaking the brim, Bogart-style, over his left eye. The look was finished by dark glasses and a soft cashmere, or fine leather bennie (a topcoat).

Richard was always color-coordinated. If dark brown was the color he was building on, he would incorporate tan, beige, and cream, right down to his underwear. He would do that with every color.

Among the Harlem peacocks, Richie was the king. Even the young turks parted like the waters of the Red Sea when he entered a place.

He was somewhat of a recluse, and moved among a more sophisticated, older crowd. It was rumored that when Richard Hill came out on the streets, something heavy was going down. In an environment where something heavy went down every day, I really didn't understand the obvious concern.

When he was on the street, new faces appeared. There was a special respect, a special deference shown towards Richard Hill, the Black Prince.

He and his crowd of older men were the founders of the Black Mafia. Most of these men had been involved with members of Murder, Incorporated in their youth. Some were now in their seventies, Richard being one of the youngest ones in the group.

We soon learned that the older men were not happy with the activities of the younger ones. There was going to be a conclave. Richard and his bodyguards showed up as the advance team a week before the other men. I was excited. I had a front row seat to what I knew would be big action, although I wasn't sure just what it involved.

I would sit with my stash of "blow," the most appropriate nickname for cocaine, on me. By now I was a coke dealer and user, so the bar was my office. Cocaine allowed me to work and party at the same time. As the tension built, I was one of the few women allowed to approach the Order of Directors, which I did with my usual flare for boldness.

I watched the show unfold. It started with Richard Hill and his main bodyguard, Frank "Red" Wright, coming into the bar around 1:00 P.M. First, Red checked out the washrooms and Richard positioned himself where he could see who was coming in. He knew from the old days of gang wars to sit a safe distance from the windows. Then he positioned another man at the exit. A third man stayed with the car at all times, and a few others were strategically placed up and down the block.

None of these guys talked to anyone. I know, I tried. They would not even answer a simple greeting.

Day after day I sat watching and waiting for my chance to get close to the Black Prince. I used this time to gather as much information about him as possible. Piecing together the bits and pieces from each person I talked to, I became familiar with his past history.

He was born in the Deep South and arrived in New York City with his mother, father and older brother Willie. They were extremely poor.

His mother worked as a domestic servant on Park Avenue. Not able to find permanent employment, Richard's father drank, gambled and soon gave up. The household became a single-parent family.

At the time, Richard was about ten-years-old. He and Willie started to steal and gradually moved up the ladder of crime. First, they ran numbers and later, beat people up for money.

Like his father before him, Willie became addicted to alcohol. In his twenties, he drank himself to death. Richard's mother, a deeply religious woman, never remarried. She prayed that drink would not claim her younger son, too. She needn't have worried. Richard was too busy with other things to care about alcohol.

Richard married twice. He and his first wife had a daughter, but were soon afterwards divorced. His second wife died. He also had a son, who lived in Florida, from a childhood girlfriend.

By the time Richard was thirty, he had been arrested for two murders—one in Boston, the other in New York. He was never convicted of either. But rumors cropped up that Richard Hill had been a mad dog killer and many unsolved murders were blamed on him.

There was one final fact on Richard Hill's life that few knew, but with my contacts, I found out: Richard Hill was a junkie.

By now, Richard Hill had accepted me as a regular. Early one day, he stopped and began to chat with me. His aide Red stood very close behind, his hand tightening on the butt of his gun, watching every move I made.

After that, they were very nice to me, always sending me drinks. A week or so later, I had a little extra money and sent drinks to them. They got a kick out of that. To me, it was good manners. I had learned my street manners from men. I had become a virago, and shared an esprit de corps with men more than with women.

It was my observation that the other women who were runners, etc., didn't know the small things. In their minds, it was uncool to buy a man a drink. That type of thinking always put them in an inferior position. I thought and operated differently because I knew I was outclassed by some of them, who were among the most gorgeous women I had ever seen.

I knew if I had to depend on my looks to get in the door, it would never open. Being honest with myself gave me another edge. I was an average-looking female who had a great body. But so did hundreds of others. And I could not bother with make-up every day like most of the girls. I had to find a different way.

I was unique, aloof, and that was the scent I put down and waited for the men to smell. Of course, it worked. I learned to use my brain everyday and my body only when I knew it would pay off, and pay off big.

I became a curiosity. Every man wanted to know about this fiercely independent child-woman.

The conclave took place over the next couple of weeks. It was decided that several members who needed discipline would be "hit." The conferees all went back to where they came from— Long Island, Connecticut, upstate New York. Afterwards, about eight high-profile killings took place. I knew some of the names, but no one personally. As for Richard, he stayed.

His punishment for being a junkie was that he was forever condemned to live among the very people he exploited. The reason he was still connected to the drug scene in a big way was that, at one time, he did some major hits on behalf of some very important people. He was allowed to stay in the Black Mafia as a major player only under certain prescribed circumstances.

One, he would always have a residence in Harlem. An on-site overseer was needed to keep an eye on investments.

Two, he was never to be seen flaunting his affliction in public by sniffling, scratching or nodding.

Three, he was always to be well-turned-out and never be confrontatirisl.

Four, he was responsible for his own staff. Bodyguards and bit players.

So there we were, Richard Hill circling me like a shark, and me slowing down long enough to get devoured. Finally, it happened. The first date was dinner at the Inn Zone, near the Polo Grounds where the hapless Mets played.

I was picked up by the bodyguard—not Red; he always stayed with Richard. It was a huge, copper-skinned man instead. He drove me to the night club, Paradise city, where I was to meet Richard for drinks.

"Miss Chickie, so glad you could make it," said Mr. Hill, holding out a chair to me. He was immaculately dressed as usual, with a big, smooth smile for me.

Paradise city had once been a fancy place. Now, the famous old girl was getting a little shabby around the edges, but she still managed to attract a colorful crowd.

As I sat sipping a Jack Daniels, people stopped by our table.

"Good evening, Mr. Hill."

"How you doin', Mr. Hill."

"So glad to see you, Mr. Hill."

As they paid their respects to Mr. Hill, the men smiled and tipped their hats and the women gestured, as if almost curtsying. This was serious respect. Richard Hill was like nobility to them, and I was basking in his long shadow.

Still, their formal manner felt awkward to me. I had never been on a real date. Now, when men swore in front of me, an apology was offered right away. Soon, I became very uncomfortable with the bowing and scraping. As for the apologies for swearing, the sides of my mouth twitched in a half smile. None of the men could match my mouth on a good day.

Later that night, as we made our entrance at the Inn Zone, some of the patrons exchanged looks of surprise and some visibly stiffened. Quickly, the manager came over.

"Oh, Mr. Hill, welcome, welcome, and your lovely lady, welcome," said the manager, turning to me, wringing his hands in a display of nervous tension. The manager had a sadistic face and thin, sardonic lips that made me think of murder. He looked as if he had absorbed an evil spirit. I shuddered.

"How are you this evening?" Richard answered nonchalantly.

"Oh, Mr. Hill, how else could I be? After all, you have honored us with your presence this evening." He added as an after thought, as if what he'd already said was not enough, "I am delighted that you have come, of course."

I wanted to laugh out loud, it was all so damn ridiculous. But something stopped me.

I edged closer to Richard to whisper my thoughts; it was then I noticed that Richard's face was also deadly serious, although I

120

had never seen him really laugh. An occasirisl crack where his lips were might have passed for a smile.

After the first date, Richard Hill phoned me every day and saw me about three times a week. Our courtship was very formal, much different than any I had known. After about two months of dating, we worked our way up to five times a week, and our first romantic kiss. By that time, my gifts from him included a Rolex, a ranch mink and a diamond ring. All the goods arrived in store boxes so that I would know they had been bought and paid for retail and not fallen off the back of a truck. He was really trying to impress me.

I was impressed, but more by his mind than his manner. In the next two months, I picked his brain for knowledge. If I was going to survive in his world, I had to protect myself with as much worldly savvy as possible.

By the end of that period, I had his apartment cleaned up and cleaned out. Painted, new furniture, drapes, the works. It wasn't easy. For some peculiar reason, he had a hard time parting with all of his junk. I later found out this was a peculiar trait of most guys. But I was firm and took on a mother's role.

To my surprise, he responded very well. Maybe he liked the idea of a new mother. At any rate, in I moved. Then I began working on him to upgrade to another building. Perhaps the Lenox Towers, a better, more modern Harlem complex, from which he could still oversee his operations. Though I tried to point out all the pluses, I could not get him to move to another building.

"No, no, no, I like it here. This is where I'm stayin'."

Richard's eyes seemed to be worsening. I convinced him to go to the doctor.

"Well frankly, Miss Chickie, I don't hold much hope. It's that pure heroin he keeps pumping into his veins," said the doctor.

"How long's he been doing it?"

"Sixteen years. I tried many times to get him to stop, but he wouldn't."

If a doctor couldn't, I knew I would have little chance to succeed. I didn't.

Richard started getting me more involved in his business. I became his eyes. Hanging with me, he was no longer a recluse and we would go out often. After all, I was a young woman and had to be shown off to society.

Show me off he did, too. It was better than a romance novel. To change clothes three times a day was a given. Looking back, I realize I could never have worn my clothes out in a lifetime. After wearing them six to ten times, I gave them to our female customers. Damned if we didn't have the best-dressed junkies in Harlem!

I finally convinced Richard to move to upstate New York. I understood that he had to keep the apartment in the city for show, but I could not live there any more. There just wasn't any room. We were being crowded out with shoes, dresses, coats and furs—mink, seal and fox. By then, Richard always sent his main man Red with me. The bodyguards, who also came along, would laugh every time Richard sent me shopping. We had to take two cars. But always looking good was only the smallest part of my value to Richard. I was also keeping his books.

A lot of his business practices changed when I came on board. I ran a tight ship. Every cent had to be accounted for.

Soon, I became one of the "Queens." Our "noble" crime family consisted of the King and Queen at the top—Richard and myself. There were four 'round the clock bodyguards—Red, Randy, Dwight and Zoot. There could be more if the need arose.

Then there were three enforcers, men capable of any type of threat and violence—up to and including murder. Thirty-five runners to push the stuff on the street, and over three-hundred customers—our street junkies. We were also acting as distributors to others outside of our organization. It was a sideline that was growing fast. The business was very profitable.

"I love this shit," said Red.

We were in a safe house, an innocuous-looking brownstone uptown, one of many where we hid the drug money.

"Yup, this is the life," continued Randy, counting out tens into a pile. There were piles and piles of money on the table that the guys were counting out.

"I'm glad you guys love your work so much. Meanwhile, pay attention," I admonished. "I want an accurate count."

When all the money was counted out, there were twenty piles, each containing five thousand dollars, all proceeds from drug sales. Red and Randy then stuffed the piles into paper bags, one pile per bag. The bags, filled to bursting, were stuffed into apple crates. Then, with one of the boys holding his gun by his side, he'd escort the other one out who'd be carrying one of the apple crates.

"How much you got in there, brothers?" a kid in T-shirt and jeans asked in front of the brownstone, as Red put the first crate in the backseat of his car. Randy looked up and down the street to make sure no one was trying a shakedown. I watched from the stoop.

The process kept up until crates filled the backseat and the trunk. Then we all piled in and were off. The crates were dropped off for safekeeping in safe houses all over the city. At any given time, we could probably put our hands on five million dollars. And we were growing larger. In fact, very soon, we became big enough to deal directly with a source country. No longer did we have to rely on a supplier for product. The negotiations began, hot and heavy.

However, it was not all growth and profit. As I was putting together a multi-million dollar internatirisl deal, I was getting some resistance from a very influential player—a tall, olive-skinned Corsican with dark features, named Vito. We needed him on our side to open some doors for us so our shipments could get through. Harbor master, customs officials, police chiefs on both sides of the ocean—their palms all had to be greased.

My plan was to give him a party he'd never forget. It would take a couple of weeks to set everything up. If I could convince Vito to work with us, it would mean millions.

How was I feeling during all this? I wasn't feeling much of anything, most of the time. Maybe I was living in denial. I was so busy with my work days and party nights that had I not been living in the lap of luxury, I would have let my own appearance go. I didn't have time to comb my hair any more, so it was off to the hair dresser every morning.

As for my coke intake, it wasn't as heavy due to the demands on my time, which now included looking after Richard. His sight had deteriorated badly, and I had to look after his every need. Angry and frustrated because of his helplessness, he had tantrums every day.

One day, he was squinting at a newspaper, trying to read it.

"Oh honey, let me, that print's too small for you to read," I said, trying to be sympathetic. I reached over to take the paper and his hand lashed out. He caught me with a vicious blow—WHAM—right across my lip, which immediately began to bleed.

"What you doin' woman? Think I'm some sort of helpless old man that needs someone to read to him?" he said with derision.

After that, anytime I got too close to him emotionally, he hit me. There were many other times.

"I told you to put five apple crates in the house on Lennox Avenue and four in the house on 114th Street, not the other way around," Richard criticized me.

"But honey, this morning— -"

WHACK! My lip began to bleed again. He settled back into his drug induced haze, certain that I had not followed his instructions to the letter.

As in any family, physical abuse was a hard thing to cover up. It was said among our family that Richard could not handle getting blind, so he took it out on me. But it was wrong of anyone, including Richard, to believe that I would accept that excuse. I was not going to be abused by anyone again, not if I could help it and certainly not by a blind, junkie gangster.

No, I would take care of that when the time was right. For the time being, I knew I had to take it in order to get what I wanted— money and power. I would swallow hard and accept every task and bruise laid upon me from the mundane— buying appropriate presents for every member of our family's birthday, based on the job they did for us and how long they had worked for us—to the important, like making sure the cops were constantly greased and kept off our necks. Inwardly, though, I kept a running tally of humiliations.

Despite my promise to myself to get even, sometimes I felt overwhelmed, and I went to my old friend, Cadillac Richie Wheeler, for advice.

"Richie, I just don't know what to do any more."

"Well Chickie, you can bail out any time."

"Not enough bread yet."

"So awright, look, keep playing to the old junkie's ego. Massage him. Tell him how great he is. And roll with his punches."

I smiled.

"No, I mean it. Look, like this."

And Richie showed me how, when somebody threw a punch at you and you couldn't avoid it, you start your face rolling away from it before it landed. That way, the brunt of the blow would be deflected.

"Thanks, boss," I said, smiling. Cadillac Richie may have been a thief and a murderer but he cared about me. Maybe it was our shared days of innocence in Vancouver. Whatever it was, he was there for me.

After our meeting, I walked out to the street, my heels clicking on the concrete. Red was waiting for me with the car.

I would never let Mr. Hill know when I met with Mr. Wheeler and Red never told on me. Politically, I'd played my cards right. I ran the business now, not Mr. Hill, and I always treated Red well. He now saw me as his boss.

Meanwhile, Richard Hill was acting like a big baby; so "Mommy," albeit sometimes with bruises, was ruling his world. And in that world, the physical abuse Mommy was subjected to was considered normal. Mommy knew better, but her angry feelings were constantly being salved by money, drugs and power. Lots of power. And I was going to gain more if my party plan was acceptable to Vito. He seemed to like it, except for one thing.

"You be my date for the evening, Chickie," Vito, the tall, swarthy but handsome Corsican insisted.

I had a friend who ran a stable I would use from time to time when we had to entertain out-of-towners. These girls entertained heads of state, mafia dons and men of the cloth. They knew their trade and loved it. I had planned to use them for Vito's amusement but he nixed the idea.

"I want you, Chickie."

Silently, I stared at him, the anger rising like bile in my throat. Who was this creep to think he could have me like some common whore? A thousand thoughts sailed through my mind, but I kept coming back to the same one.

How bad did I want this deal? My answer came quick. Real bad. This was going to make me enough money—my share would be over 1 million dollars. With that, I could get away from Richard.

"Okay," I told Vito. "I'll be your date."

The date was made for a weeknight, and we would stay in, out of the limelight.

I had been thinking about my escape for months. Now I began to formulate my plans. When Richard had to spend all day at the clinic with his doctors, I started to pack up belongings in boxes. I sent some of my clothes to my girlfriend Trina.

"I'm just sending the stuff to my poor relatives in Nova Scotia," I lied when Richard came home early once and asked what I was doing.

It was impossible to pack up everything, I had so much, but I put my most valuable furs in a vault for storage. Richard did not know where. I kept a record of each mink, sable, chinchilla and Russian broadtail.

The most valuable pieces of jewelry were sent to jewelers, ostensibly for cleaning. Meanwhile, I kept all the claim checks on me. No way was I going to get conned out of my valuables. Richard looked at them all as gifts. I saw them as well-earned pay.

The plan was set. Now all I had to do was execute it.

Vito's apartment was located on the East Side in one of Manhattan's better neighborhoods. I planned the meal, catered by La Saison, and picked up the tab. Everything was on me. I even brought with me green orchids for the table to add to the many floral arrangements I had sent ahead.

"Chickie, you really thought of everything," Vito said with an admiring smile.

I knew that Vito's favorite drink was Napoleon Brandy. A case of twenty-five year old brandy was sent ahead. Nothing, and I mean nothing, was left to chance.

"I feel I should have done more," he told me, coming over and running his hand down my bare back. I wore a Chanel creation with a plunging neckline and a scoop back, all in elegant black silk.

"Well darling," I purred, "you could select the music." With that, Vito gracefully strolled across the large, luxurious living room.

Beige velvet wallpaper led up the walls to scalloped mahogany moldings. A few original French oils and some well done copies looked down at us. There was a mahogany breakfront and country French antiques scattered about on elegantly styled tables, and plush sofas and loveseats covered in various shades of blue velvet.

Vito put a record on the stereo. Enrico Caruso's melodious tenor floated through the rooms, stroking my ears with extraordinary beauty. Vito had some taste after all. Maybe he wouldn't be so hard to take. It might be a fun evening after all.

After a few drinks, we got up to dance. Vito was light on his feet. I complimented him on his dancing.

"We took lessons together."

Not yet wondering who "we" was, I looked around again as I danced with him. The place was nicely furnished all right, but there were no human touches, no pictures of family, things like that.

"Do you live here full time?" I asked.

"No, we live on an old estate on Long Island's north shore."

"Who's this 'we' you keep mentioning?"

"The wife and kids."

What he didn't say was what the old, moneyed Long Island gentry would say if they knew they had a big-time drug dealer living next door to them. As for his loving wife, ten to one she did not know about this apartment.

"Does she know about this apartment?"

"Of course not."

They never did. A bitter feeling filled my stomach. As long as these men pampered them with every human luxury and life-long memberships to this or that, private schools for the kids and fabulous holidays, they would never ask an inappropriate question.

"What is your wife like, Vito?"

He sighed. "She complains about everything."

"Neurotic, huh?"

"Very.

I hated those women. You could build them a castle, they could have real estate coming out the old wazoo and they still would not be happy. One thing about street women I told myself: they are not afraid to work side by side with their men and get their hands dirty.

We ate dinner with a Puccini aria floating in the background. After dinner, Napoleon brandy, a Cuban cigar for Vito and a few shared lines of the best Bolivian Flake. Then he led me to his bedroom. We walked through French doors. Even though we were weren't in a hotel room, I closed the bedroom doors out of habit.

The bed was a king size four poster with blue velvet bedspread and peach satin sheets. There was a 19th Century oak chest on top of which was an old style wash basin, and twin oak bed tables.

Lying on the bed, we began making love. Vito had wired the room with speakers, and Caruso was helping us to realize our passion. Vito, though, did not need much help. He was very excited, but trying very hard to please me. When he could contain himself no longer, he mounted me, all the while stroking my ego with sweet pillow talk. I smiled up at him, sure I had the deal.

Suddenly, the French doors burst open. No time to get him off me, I tried to look over Vito's shoulder, but he had me pinned to the bed while his hot fluid pumped into me.

PHHT.

It was a low, quiet sound, and Vito stopped pumping. I felt grit and wet stuff on the side of my face and upper body. I brought my hand up to wipe some away. Then, I saw it. The grit was skull fragments and the wet stuff brains and blood. My scream was drowned out in Caruso's crescendo.

My life didn't flash before my eyes as many people near death report. No time for that shit. There was no doubt in my mind that this was a hit, and probably a professional shooter. If so, the shooter had to take me out. too. I needed to act quickly. I pushed the dead weight of Vito's body off me. I started to talk fast.

"Now listen, baby. I do *not* know you. I have *not* seen you, and I *don't* care about the stiff," I said, looking down at Vito's lifeless eyes and up at the coal black ones of his killer. "We were just having some fun. Them's the breaks. If he had a hit on him, then so be it. It's got nothing to do with me. I'm just gonna get dressed and get the fuck outa here. I'm not even going to the bathroom to clean up, I'll just wipe my face with the clean end of the sheet here and be on my way. You had to do your job and

I'm all for that. You don't ever have to worry about me, ever. Please mister, if you never gave a person a break before, you're overdue. I see you have gloves on. Very good. Don't forget to get rid of the silencer right away. I know you've got everything covered but never get caught with a silencer."

I said all that and more, all in one breath, dressing at the same time. I was shaking so much, I put my dress on backwards.

If that man was going to shoot me, it would be for talking too much—but I couldn't stop. My life depended on it! "Don't say anything because I don't want to hear your voice. Signal me who should leave first."

The killer with the coal black eyes said nothing.

I pointed to myself with my finger toward my chest. I was shocked to see him nod, move out of the doorway and with a sweeping gesture and a very faint smile on his grim face, bow me out of the room.

My body numb, my heart beating out of control, I walked. I was not going to run. I closed the doors ever so gently, still waiting for the bullet to come crashing into my spine.

When I hit the street, I got mad.

Laughing and crying at the same time, I talked to myself. Dammit. Look at me. I must look like hell. I'm covered with a dead man's brains and blood. My whole body's shaking. What if the police see me? Good thing I remembered to take my purse. I sure hope I got most of it off. What I'm gonna do to that shooter if I ever see him again is indescribable, and I *will* see him again. But then I'll be in the driver's seat. It'll be his blood and brains that are splattered.

I'd walked about ten blocks, raising hell, when I slowed down long enough to grab a taxi.

"Take me to 92nd and York."

That's where my girlfriend Trina had her place. She could be trusted. She never asked me any questions.

"Oh, Chickie," Trina said as she opened the door to her apartment. She motioned me in.

"I want to take a bath. Quick."

"Go."

I took a long, hot, bath and scrubbed and scrubbed. I washed my hair at least five times. Then I got under the shower and rinsed until my skin was pink and puckered like a newborn's.

Trina and I were the same size, so I put on fresh clothes.

"Get me some garbage bags."

It struck me that the last time I'd handled paper bags was to put money in them. Now I was reduced to filling them with blood-stained clothes.

"Come on."

"Where we goin'?" Trina asked.

"To run an errand."

The street was dark and deserted. That made our task easier. We walked around the neighborhood putting the bags in different garbage cans.

Trina never asked, and I never told her a thing. I'm sure to this day she thinks I killed someone and she helped me get rid of the evidence.

We went back to her house and got drunk. I called Richard and told him, "I finished my business early and I'm going to visit my girlfriend for awhile." Richard laughed and said, "Have a good time. Don't get in any trouble. You shoulda had Red pick you up. I worry when you're out there alone."

If only he knew.

CHAPTER EIGHT

Getting out

Richard's behavior was getting worse. He'd started to pull guns on me in the house. Everyone would run because, by now, he was almost blind. I would just stand there, wishing he would put me away.

I was burnt out. I tried to tell Richard that I needed a rest, that I was thinking of going to Nova Scotia to get my head together.

A close encounter with death is not a good thing to face when you're trying to live in denial, and mine with Pepe had been traumatic. Despite all the money and power, I now had that moment to live with, the one between life and death, where your life hangs in the balance. It had caused me to stare firsthand down the barrel of the shooter's silencer, at the brutality of the life I was living and the realization made me want to die.

I was a gangster's woman, nothing more than a two-bit gun moll. People didn't respect me, they feared me or they hung around me hoping to get some action. I didn't have any real friends. Oh, we called each other friends but none of us ever trusted the other enough to form a real bond.

If we weren't drunk, we were stoned or so busy trying to out-dress, out-eat and out do each other in every way. The junkies, they were getting younger. Hell, I would fire one of our people for selling drugs to a child, not realizing that I was making it happen no matter what I said. As long as the drug was on the streets,

133

kids could get to it. Twenty-year-old junkies would buy a bundle and sell half a fix to a twelve-year-old. How would I ever know? The papers had accounts in it every day of children dying of overdoses on the city streets.

I couldn't help wondering, did those kids die on my stuff?

And after what had happened in Pepe's apartment, I couldn't get my head together. Why was I always being spared? Couldn't I die? A lot of the time, I wanted to.

I started to hate Richard, but how could I leave him? He was blind. I tried to get him to kick his habit, but the doctor said he would die. It would kill him. The shock would be too hard on his heart.

Meanwhile, the drug wars had hit hard. Every day, people were getting ripped off and gunned down on the streets. The city was getting to be very dangerous.

"Let's close up shop and run, stay out of town for awhile," I said.

God knows we had enough cash. Richard, though, didn't want to leave. He was worried about his people, Red the most. Even though by this time he was treating Red very badly. He would grab Red's arm and beat his face and head. Red would never hit back.

Richard was very cruel. I think that's why his people liked working for me. But even I could only control him to a minimum extent. In private, he was still abusing me, too.

The bars we frequented were shadowy, with very little natural light and very dim bulbs. All to create atmosphere. You had to stop at the entrance in order to adjust your eyes if it was a bright, sunny day outside.

One such June day, one of Cadillac Richie's boys, Junior, came into the bar. Tall, muscular, honey-skinned, he was young, good-looking and always polite. He was a little bit like Cadillac Richie. People had begun noticing and talking about Junior. He was a new star and anxious to make his reputation.

Junior strode into the bar from the bright outdoors and blearily walked—slam bang—into Richard Hill. Richard, standing in the shadows, being jet black in all dark clothing, it was understandable to everyone except Richard that Junior had stumbled into him. Richard lost his mind.

"You son-of-a-bitch, motherfucka!"

He became an hysterical fishwife, screeching, screaming, foaming at the mouth and stamping his feet in anger. Junior tried in vain to appease him.

"Mr. Hill, please I'm sor—"

"You lousy cock sucker . . ."

"Look, Mr. Hill, I didn't mean—"

"Stick it up your ass, you dickhead."

Richard would not listen to any reason. Finally, Junior walked away from him, not wishing to be abused any longer. Almost under his breath, he said, "That little black nigger is crazy."

Richard heard.

"Red, I want you to shoot that bastard right here and right now!" Richard ordered.

Red looked over at me. I shook my head.

"No, Mr. Hill, I won't."

"Red, you're fired."

Nothing unusual there. Richard did that often.

After Richard cooled down, I took him home, gave him his fix—a job that Red almost always did for Richard, and I didn't like to do. Of course, Richard and Red "made up" later.

After we got Richard in the bed and he was on the nod, I went out looking for Junior. I had to do some damage control. I found him and we talked for about an hour.

"Look," Junior finally said, "if that little nigger apologizes to me publicly in the same bar, I'll consider it over."

"Okay," I promised, "you'll get what you want."

The last thing we needed was a gang war with Cadillac Richie.

This was going to be hard. I waited until the next day to reason with "Crazy" Richard, as people were now calling him.

"Richard," I said reasonably, "if the bosses hear another of your outburst—"

"Outburst, what—"

"Just listen. If they hear about it, it's not going to make them happy."

He heard me. He was supposed to maintain a low profile and he hadn't. The last thing he wanted to do was bring the wrath of the Mafia down on his head.

"Sometimes, honey," I said soothingly, "a person has to apologize for their own sake and the sake of their family. After all, a lot of people could get hurt over a mistake."

I didn't know how he'd take my suggestion, but to my surprise, he agreed. I made the phone call and a time and place was set up for the two men to meet.

There was one, big thing that needed to be dealt with. Even though Richard was going to apologize, he couldn't lose face. It was going to be a difficult discussion.

We called in eight family members. With the three of us, that made eleven strong. We dressed with care and all of us carried guns, including me. Though in my case, it might not have been the best idea.

I was dangerous with a gun, because I hadn't mastered the art of shooting. Red and the boys tried to teach me gun control, but just as I had trouble learning discipline in other areas of my life, I had trouble with this one too. I was too wild.

"Maybe you shouldn't carry a gun Chickie," Red warned. "Remember your foot."

I was so bad with a gun that I once shot myself in the foot instead of hitting the target.

"No way," I said, all pumped up. "You guys pack, I pack."

So off we went.

In doorways across the street from the bar where we were to meet, The Shanty, Junior and his boys stood waiting impatiently. There were ten of them, all well-dressed, but a few of them had clothes that did nothing to conceal the bulges under their armpits. They were not going inside in case of an ambush. When they saw us coming, they stepped out onto the sidewalk and came to meet us halfway.

We all looked at each other. No one said anything. It was sizing up time. Then Richard stepped forward with his right hand outstretched. Junior took it with a strong grip and they shook hands. After that, there was handshaking all around as one of our boys paired off with one of theirs and so on. With the preliminaries over, it was time to seal the truce with a drink.

In the bar, the drinks were on the house. The owner knew how to work the room and get people in the mood. After a few shots of Jack Daniels, without any hurry in his step, Richard walked over to Junior.

"I'm real sorry for the way I acted the other day," he said very sincerely.

"Apology accepted," Junior replied.

Then someone started up the jukebox, girls emerged from wherever they'd been hiding, and a party began. Pretty soon, amid the rush of good feelings from the booze and the increased libidos in the room, the dispute was forgotten and pleasure was once again the imperative.

Cadillac Richie Wheeler waded through the crowd which seemed to part in the middle by his very presence. He pulled me aside. "You did good, kid," he said with a smile.

Damn right I did. I knew Junior's character now. From now on, I would not walk too close to Cadillac Richie.

After that, Richard, Red and I took off for Nova Scotia. That lasted about three months.

Poor Red had to go back to the city every month to bring Richard his drugs. He could have brought enough in for a year with one visit, but Richard would have lost control of him. So he made Red travel back and forth each time, running the risk of being busted at the border. But Richard didn't care about the risks Red took, only that he would have the right stuff when he wanted and needed it. Besides, if Richard ran out, he was only a few hours by plane from the streets of New York.

As I watched Red service his boss, I realized that I couldn't stay with Mr. Hill. I'd put my time in, paid my dues, almost been killed.

I wanted out.

In Nova Scotia, I had time to think, and I began thinking about my old employer, Leo Valenti. I had never forgotten him or any of them who made me eat dirt. I talked to Cadillac Richie about doing the biggest score ever—ripping off Leo Valenti.

I knew Leo never put head to pillow without knowing where every penny was stashed. In addition, he also never made a move without an army of bodyguards. I was sure we could work out a surprise for Valenti.

I needed a lot of money, more money than I had access to with Mr. Hill. There was one proviso: I couldn't steal from the family to whom I was loyal. But in order for me to get away from Richard Hill, I had to put my hands on a lot of cash.

Hell, I was used to fine living and didn't want to give that up. Ever. I also knew that I would have to stay out of sight for at least two to five years so Mr. Hill would stop looking for me. In that time, I needed more than my talent at mimic and disguise. I would get plastic surgery to completely change my appearance. When the time was right, I'd reappear, open a business, maybe a nice restaurant and bar, meet a guy and get married.

In my fantasies, I was just an old-fashioned girl, but one that wanted to be well off. I was also desperate. That was reality.

I had to have money. I was not trained, had no education or skills that could transfer into the legitimate sector. Besides, even if I had, who'd hire an ex-con with a record like mine? There was no use carrying my fantasies to extremes. In order for me to make it, I had to start out with big bucks. So, I got on the line with Cadillac Richie and told him that I wanted to rip off Leo Valenti.

"Are you out of your mind!? You better leave that one alone," he said succinctly.

And no matter how I presented the plan to Cadillac Richie he wasn't going for it.

"Chickie, if you want to get out and leave that nigger you're with, come back to New York and I'll put you under my protection and back you in a little bar. But under no circumstances will I entertain doing Leo Valenti.

"Remember, this Chickie," Richie continued. "Never go after a man that's not afraid to die. And Leo fits that description to a T. In order to rob him, you'd have to kill him and all his people. He's got some crazy muthafuckas working for him. You'd have to take them all out."

After listening to Cadillac Richie, I decided he was probably right about Valenti. I was even more sure he was dead wrong about Richard Hill. Hill would never leave me alone if I was in New York.

Since I was running everything now, if he lost me, he would lose most of his family and his business. I also knew too much. No way he could trust me because I could use all the information against him, and run him out of business. I'd never have done that, but he didn't know that and it wouldn't have made any difference if he did.

All Richard Hill had to look forward to if I left him was the life of a blind street junkie. He was long past his prime and had burnt all his bridges to the ground. With me gone, there'd be nothing left to lose. He'd use his last dollar to hunt me down like a rabid dog and kill me himself or have me whacked. As for Cadillac Richie's protection, it wouldn't be enough. Bottom line: Richard Hill was crazy.

I thought and thought about solutions. Finally, I decided on one. I'd cook up more dope than was needed for his next shot, and put him out of his misery. What did he have to look forward to? If Red left him, that would be the end of him. Then again, I didn't know how much to cook in order to kill him. Richard was using enough dope to kill five junkies as it was, and the stuff was almost pure.

Thinking like that stopped me from doing it. Besides, was I tough enough, ruthless enough, animal enough, conscienceless enough to do a hands-on murder? Just cold-blooded like that?

No, my conscience answered.

Finally, I decided on a course of action that might buy me my life.

Red would just have to take Richard back with him the next time he came to Nova Scotia. I phoned Red and got him on the line.

"Listen Red," I said, "I know you're not due for awhile, but I need you to come now, no questions asked, and call me when you get within fifty miles."

"Okay Chickie, I got it" said Red.

"And one more thing," I added. "I'm leaving and I won't be here when you get here, which is why the phone call before-hand is necessary."

Even though I knew I had to move quickly, I didn't want to leave Richard alone in the house for very long. After all, he was blind and an addict.

As soon as I got the call from Red a few days later, I gave Richard his last fix from me. God, he was so trusting, like a little baby. Walking out with the clothes on my back and whatever money I could scrape together, I left him.

That was the last time I saw Richard Hill. I pulled the claim checks out of my purse and sent for my furs and jewelry. When I got them I pawned them, for a grand total of ten cents on the dollar. With my lifestyle, the money didn't last very long and soon I was broke. The bulk of my stuff was still back in New York at Richard Hill's apartment, and I couldn't get it without putting myself in jeopardy.

I still worried about that old junkie; so from time to time, as I tried to lose myself in different places on both sides of the border, I phoned Red to see how things were going. One day, Red replied, "Things are bad. The new wiseguys'll have nothing to do with Mr. Hill, because all he did in the old days was throw up in their faces."

"Does he go out much?" I asked Red.

"Not really, but when he does, he goes in the bars, takes his gun out and shoots in the air."

"Red, you ought to take what's left of the money and put Richard in a nice home, then you can get work with Cadillac Richie. I'll make the phone call myself on your behalf."

"No way," Red said with determination. He would hang in with Richard.

I felt badly, but I realized Red wasn't too smart, which was why he'd sacrificed whatever he could have done with his life on the altar of Richard's drug habit. And the drug he regularly pumped into his own veins left him too shortsighted to see the handwriting on the wall. I could, though, and didnot call him again until two years later, when I called to talk withTrina, my old girlfriend.

"Happy to hear from you Chickie," Trina greeted me warmly across the many miles. "Ya know what's happenin'?"

I confessed I didn't.

"Your old friend Richard Hill and Red Wright got shot down, gangland style, in front of the same bar where the meeting of the Mafia bosses occurred a while back."

"Why'd they kill 'em?"

"No reason was given," she said cryptically.

"What about Cadillac Richie?"

She laughed. "Oh, he made The New York Times. Hold on, I'll get the article. I thought you might call and I saved it for you."

There was a pause on the line, then she came back and began to read:

Police and 4 Men Exchange 50 Shots

"An exchange of more than 50 shots among four plainclothes men and four men who opened fire on them early yesterday sent Dwayne Q. Fisher, 25 years old, to Columbia Presbyterian Medical Center with a head wound. "His condition was later described as poor."

"Charges of attempted murder of police officers and possession of deadly weapons were placed against the victim and Richard Wheeler, 36, and Stephen O'Neil, 34. One man escaped. "The policemen said they were answering what later proved to be a false report of a stabbing when they saw four men in a parked car.

"When two of the men got out and peered into the door of a tavern on the corner, the police said, they left their own unmarked car to investigate a possible holdup. They were greeted with gunfire from all four suspects, they reported, and returned fire after identifying themselves as the police.

"Cadillac Richie has lawyers on retainer just for contingencies like this. He was probably out on bail within twenty four hours," I said.

Richard Wheeler was nothing if not colorful. I later learned he made The New York Times one more time that same year.

Man Seized in Slaying of Bronx Drug Processor

A suspected gangland assassin for a narcotics syndicate was held on $250,000 bail yesterday on an indictment charging him with the murder of a reputed narcotics "factory" operator and his bodyguard.

The suspect, Raymond Lopez, was arrested in East Meadow, L.I. and charged with illegal possession of a revolver and a live hand grenade on Tuesday. He was picked up and brought back yesterday on a warrant. At that time, District Attorney Anthony D. Falcone announced the indictment handed up last May. The indictment alleges that the suspect was one of three men who shot and killed Richard Wheeler, 36 years old, and Herman Travers, 26, last Feb. 3.

Mr. Falcone said that Wheeler had been the operator of a major heroin processing factory. He said the indictment alleges that the suspect, along with two accomplices still being sought, shot Wheeler in the head as he started to get into a Cadillac, parked in front of his home. The prosecutor said that the three then shot Travers, who was at the wheel of the car. Mr. Falcone said the shooting was one of several incidents last February that have been traced to friction between gangs involved in narcotics. Lopez was arraigned before Justice Finnian Ryan. A hearing was set for Monday.

I also discovered what the article didn't say: Raymond Lopez, Cadillac Richie's new bodyguard, wanted to do more than guard the prince. He wanted control.

Lopez was a Vietnam vet who had just returned home, and Richie had given him a break because he had all this special forces training. Richie figured to get that power on his side. It turned on him instead.

So Richard Wheeler and Richard Hill were dead. My two mentors. I didn't feel much of anything. I had said my goodbyes years before.

CHAPTER NINE

The Mad Bomber

I reverted to my past life, but nothing gave me a thrill—drugs, sex, criminal actions, nothing. My will to live was lost. I just didn't care. As for friends, I still had none. Those people I saw were bottom-feeders just like me, road kill and beneath contempt. I mixed drugs—mescaline, LSD, speed, coke, all kinds of pills.

All across North America, I woke up in dirty rooms and staggered into a noonday sun, leaving some strange man who'd picked me up the night before. I never saw any of them again.

I stole anything I could turn into money. I had no choice. I was very dirty and always stoned. I now had the vacant eyes and drooling mouth of a committed junkie.

I remembered how, as a very young girl a hundred years before, I was always clean. I hated being dirty. In those days when I traveled, I would stop at gas stations and wash from head to toe. Now, I couldn't even remember when I'd last had a bath.

Back in Canada again, I made it as far as the West Coast and Vancouver, where I started to have drug seizures. One day, I collapsed on the streets. People passed by. No one paid attention to me because deadbeats were very common in the part of the city I was hanging out in. That part of the city bordered Chinatown and the red light district. The heroin addicts stayed close to Chinatown, because any smack coming into Vancouver was under the control of the Chinese at that time.

145

Sometimes, I would stand for hours watching the fat cats in their big, new cars and fine clothes, with their beautiful young women. There was something very familiar about what I was seeing, but somehow I couldn't bring it into focus.

When these high rollers walked close, they pointed to me disdainfully:

"You're a pitiful sight."

"Why don't you get a job, you fucking junkie."

"You're disgusting."

"Somebody ought to shoot you and put you out of your misery."

The women would throw their heads back and laugh.

As more time went by, my situation grew worse. Now, the gutter was my home. I was as sooty and filthy as the streets. I was a bag lady. I had long forgotten what day it was or where I lay. All I knew was that I was hungry and filthy. Then one rainy afternoon, time stopped. There was only space. Sometime later, I woke up, not knowing where I was but I knew I wanted to stay in this new place. I felt clean and I was in a clean bed. Soft voices spoke. They were very close to me. My thinking still was not crystal clear, but I was awake and oh, so hungry.

I felt something in my arm. Slowly, my eyes opened. They focused on what it was that was attached to my arm. It was an I.V.

"She's awake," said a man's voice.

"That was a close one," a woman replied.

"She's not out of the woods yet," the man countered.

My thoughts faded. I slept again. Days later when I awoke, I learned I was in a hospital ward. I soon found out that after overdosing, I'd passed out in the gutter. My body was sprawled in the street. Any passing car could have killed me. Instead, I got lucky. A guy picked me up and called an ambulance. A white-clothes ghost who passed said, "That was three days ago."

I nodded. Now, I was encased in clean, white sheets in a hospital bed. A young, white coated man with thick red hair leaned over me.

"You have kidney and bladder infections, v.d., body lice, skin rashes and some motor difficulty," the attending physician informed me in an unemotional voice. "You'll have to stay in the hospital for a few more tests."

"Fine with me," I said sleepily, and sighed.

Nestling in my cocoon. Clean sheets and blankets. Three squares a day. What could be bad? A week later, the same doctor came in to see me.

"Look Dorothy," he began, "you still have some residual infection; so we're going to ask you to take antibiotics."

I nodded.

"And your motor skills might take a while to return," he added in a distorted tone. "Now I don't want to tell you how to live your life but if you want to stay alive, you better stay away from drugs and drink and take better care of yourself."

"I understand," I said, nodding again, wondering how in the hell this inexperienced, naive guy expected me to do that.

The next morning, the nurse gave me some new clothes, and I was released from the hospital.

They gave me a slip of paper with the name and address of a street organization, and told me to get a job. Doing what? I still wondered. Without an education or skills, how was I supposed to get work? Of course I went back on the streets—where else was I going to go?

Once again, I started to sell drugs; I promised myself that this time, I'd make just enough to live on. I hung around this cafe downtown that was my unofficial headquarters.

"Hey Chickie, how ya doin?"

"Fine, David."

David McVay was one of my customers.

"Interested in getting into some new stuff?"

I was a little wary. How did I know he wasn't an undercover? But gradually, over time, I checked out his pedigree with my street contacts and found out he was legit.

David belonged to a theft ring that only dealt in high quality merchandise—art, bonds and antiques. They'd steal the goods in Canada and sell some of the more traceable stuff in the States. Cheap goods were fenced on the local market, furs and jewelry in Chinatown.

The Chinese had their own people, the Triad, to take care of resetting the jewelry and remodeling the furs. By the time the Triad crafts people were through, the original owners would never recognize the goods if they passed them on the street, which some did. I decided this was a good time to reactivate my Chinese persona and took back the name Mah May Wan.

Stolen art had a select clientele. If you had to characterize robbery by its level of sophistication, art thievery would be the most sophisticated end of the business. I found the art thieves underground network fascinating in its intellectual variety. Most of them came from the aristocracy and became rogue black sheep due mostly to scandal and disinheritance.

"Those guys have a great background, but if you want to get it done, you call a man from the street," David McVay would often tell me.

True art thieves thought of their profession as a craft. They loved the excitement of putting a plan together and beating the odds. David, though, was not an aristocrat. Far from it. He was a street kid, like me, a smash and grab kind of guy, in it just for the money.

David showed me some of the loot he'd grabbed. As I gazed at the fine paintings, jewelry and furs in the apartment he used as his storehouse, my dormant sense of greed arose. I wanted to possess them. I was tired of being down and out. But I didn't have the money to pay. We worked out a deal.

David belonged to a gang of about ten men and women. This group was hot. They were going out every second day and bringing in large hauls of swag. All of them loved to party with coke after a score.

148

"You can have your pick of whatever you want, Wan," David promised, "if you'd get us some coke."

That was easy enough. All the Chinatown players knew me. Henry Lu, one of the biggest coke dealers, was more than happy to give me two ounces on consignment. I sold it to David and his friends for four thousand dollars, kept a thousand for myself as commission, and gave Henry the rest. Everyone was happy, and David invited me to all his parties, which was how I met one of this group's oddest members: Sammy the Bomber.

I never asked any questions but was soon told what was happening for my own safety.

"Sammy's a crazy man," David said soberly. Indeed he was. He made Richard Hill look sane.

Sammy was a sixty-five-year-old demolitions expert and locksmith who had gone mad and turned to a life of crime. In the process, he became invaluable to the underworld. His rap sheet stretched from New York to Toronto. A skinny little balding runt, he wore baggy clothes and wire-rimmed glasses. The overall effect was to downplay what he really was: one of the most dangerous men alive.

Sammy walked around wired with plastic explosives. The explosives were wired to a motion detonator. You couldn't slap him on the back in a greeting, or shake his hand too vigorously, or make any sudden moves that would cause Sammy to blow up and take us all with him.

The police knew about Sammy's explosive tendencies. They were ordered never to give chase to Sammy's car because, if an accident occurred, he would blow up and take out five city blocks with him.

The trunk was where he stored most of his explosives. He also had the car wired. And if you happened to visit Sammy, you had to phone ahead and see if he wanted company because his whole house was booby-trapped. I didn't care. What the hell, if I wanted to visit somebody, I showed up.

"Boy Wan, you're just as crazy as me," Sammy said admiringly.

"No one's as crazy as you," I answered, smiling.

"True, true," he said seriously, then broke down with a wide grin and started laughing.

We hit it off, two kindred, crazy spirits.

"Want to learn a little about the business?"

"Does that mean I have to go around wired like you?"

"You're not as crazy as me."

"I can try."

Sammy began to take me on scores.

Both dressed in black, we were outside a deserted building near the center of town at two in the morning. Sammy carried a bag. From it he extracted a few items and began working on a carefully camouflaged box in the back of the building. I heard the sound of wires being cut.

"Okay, Wan, the alarm's disconnected. Do your thing."

I shinnied up a drain pipe, to the fire escape, then ran up it to the roof. Over the roof to the entrance door, which I jimmied open with a screwdriver I took from my pants pocket. Down the stairs to the bottom, where I let Sammy in. Swiftly, he closed the door.

We were in a jewelry store. Running to the back, we found the safe. Sammy had cased the place in the previous few days so he knew where everything would be.

Once again into the bag, out with plastic, blasting cap and detonator. With the dexterity of a man who'd been doing the same thing all his life, Sammy put it all together and attached it to the door of the safe.

"Here, give me some help with this," and Sammy and I threw over a desk. Taking refuge behind it, Sammy very politely handed me some cotton plugs.

"Better for your ears," he said, stuffing his in the ear canals.

Sammy pushed a button and the safe exploded with a loud boom and a rush of air. Quickly, we vaulted over the desk, ran into the safe, emptied the drawers of jewels into nylon bags we took from our pockets, then scrammed through the front door.

"If the cops are around, we're shot anyway so why go through the rigmarole of going back to the roof and down again," Sammy advised.

Seeing the street still deserted, Sammy continued, "Okay, we're fine; now Wan, about that shortcut . . ."

Sammy followed me across the street and down a few blocks into Chinatown. I had arranged a shortcut for us through Triad territory. We cut through kitchens, underground tunnels and other places that only the respected few knew about and were allowed into.

We emerged under the night sky halfway across town. Even if someone had been following us, there was no way they could pick up our trail. And since we'd gone on foot, there would be no description of a getaway car.

I arranged safe passage through Chinatown a couple of times. We never got caught.

Sometimes, if we were breaking into a place in a more populated district where the chances of being discovered in the act were that much greater, we'd arrive at a score with a truck and steal the safe because it was too dangerous to blow on the premises. When we got to our safe house, the peeling would begin.

"Watch," Sammy advised, banging a sledge hammer against the side of the safe.

"The idea is to hit—" and Sammy struck the corner of the safe away from the hinges—" the stress point."

"What happens?"

"Watch," he repeated.

After a few more strokes, the steel at the point of impact began to peel away. Underneath was another layer of the hard stuff.

"Again," he shouted, and struck. Sweat poured down his neck, but soon, another layer of steel had peeled away.

"How many of those layers we got to get through before we get in?"

"Oh, about ten or twenty," he said smiling. "Here, you try," and he extended the sledge hammer.

I tried hitting for awhile, but I was never able to do a good job peeling a safe because the sledgehammer was too heavy for me. My arms felt like they were falling off after four swings. Just when I was beginning to think that we were going to have to take turns spelling each other, two other guys arrived to help out. By then I was soaked.

"Son-of-a-bitch."

"Hey, Wan, everything's an experience," and Sammy smiled.

Sammy also taught me how to circumvent very sophisticated alarm systems. Man, I loved this stuff at first. But like always, I was getting bored. Sammy knew that I needed some new thrills and suggested I go out and blow something up just for fun and practice.

"If you're gonna do stuff just to get your rocks off," Sammy preached like the professor he was, "don't waste materials. Flame and paper can be enough. You also don't want to tip the cops by getting too sophisticated unless you have to. And never blow something up without a reason, even for fun."

Armed with this bit of philosophy, I went to a local bar, the Dublin Pub, and had a beer. Now what could I blow up and have some fun with?

After a few hours, Slasher walked in. Slasher barely topped five feet and weighed eighty pounds soaking wet. He was Chinese, with long black hair and tinted John Lennon glasses that he thought made him look real cool.

"Heard the latest cut by the Stones?" Slasher asked.

Slasher and I talked rock music all the time. Behind the hippie veneer, though, was a son-of-a-bitch with a vicious temper who liked to beat people up. It was rumored he'd bumped off a couple of people. And that's when I knew what I'd blow up.

The way I figured it, if you walked around with a name like Slasher, you should be prepared to be challenged.

"And don't forget to always use good technique," Sammy admonished me the following night.

Good technique. Off I went at 2:00 A.M. with old Sammy's blessings. I found the car where I knew it would be parked. Breaking the window, I tossed in the newspapers, doused them with lighter fluid and threw in the match. It lit with a whoosh.

I'd put a block between me and the car when I heard the loud bang as the fire hit the gas tank and the car blew up. I must have had the widest grin in existence at that point painted across my face. Boy, did I feel good! Then I noticed that the sparks from the explosion were spreading to a nearby wood frame house.

I drove to a pay phone.

"Hello, Slasher?"

"Hello?"

"Slasher, get the fuck out of your house. It's going to catch on fire."

"Wan?" he said. "Is that you, Wan?"

"Yes man, get the hell out."

As he hung up, I could hear him say "What the fuck!"

I stayed close by until the fire department came and put the fire out. I never hid. I saw Slasher two days later and told him why I'd done it. He just looked at me and shook his head.

"You're . . . dangerous," was all he could muster.

Not the first time that was said, and not the last. After that, I took on the characteristics of my mentor, crazy Sammy. I walked around with a valise full of all kinds of liquid explosives, blasting caps, wires and plastic explosive. When people who knew what I was carrying saw me, they'd scream and duck for cover. I just stood there laughing because if that valise blew, screaming, ducking, and running wasn't going to help.

As my reputation as the mad bomber grew, I got into coke again. That moved me into a crazier group of thieves. I felt like all these strange people inside my head were gnawing at me, telling me what to do, fighting for attention, making demands on my life. The drugs were mastering me. I couldn't reason. I was so far gone by then, all I wanted was peace, but I didn't know where to find it.

The self-loathing which had begun so long ago grew intense. I still hung out with my gang in the bars, but I was no longer impressed with their stories. Nothing I saw or heard helped me make any sense of what I felt.

For the first time in my life, I began to look at myself. I was living like a rabid dog. Running around and around in circles, getting into all kinds of trouble and causing trouble and death for others. I had to turn this around. I just had to.

I became quieter, more withdrawn. The people who hung out with me kept asking if I was depressed. I shook my head but said nothing.

Day by day, still living in the same environment, I stayed in the game, but only enough to buy something to drink, pay my room and eat.

So there I was, lost in the wilderness.

One summer day, I was feeling particularly depressed, not having slept for days. Ordinarily, I could never trust my true feelings. Were they drug-induced? A result of the pathetic gene pool I'd been born into? The weather? P.M.S.? Because I never knew, I would just ignore everything I felt. But this day, this day was different. I couldn't ignore my feelings.

I felt my lifetime cocktail had been mixed of three parts anger, two parts hate and one part depression. Now, my senses seemed heightened.

As I walked along the streets, looking into the tortured faces of the street people, I felt for the first time that I was responsible for some of their pain. My own pain was so intense, a groan escaped aloud.

My steps quickened. I ran to the place where I was staying. rushed inside and let myself into my room. Then, I threw myself on the bed and lay there spread-eagled.

My body felt like it was held rigid. I couldn't move. I closed my eyes and fell into unconsciousness. A rogue's gallery of all the gangsters I knew passed in front of me. All dead, all in torment. Babies just being born and young children were before me, reaching out their hands towards me. They were sinking into swamps as deep and as cold as the Canadian tundra. "Help, help," they cried in silent appeal, but they were all bogged down and I couldn't help. Oh, I so desperately wanted to; but I was rooted to the spot.

This went on for two days. Then, as quickly as it came upon me, it left.

When it was over, I tried to dismiss it all as a bad dream.

Man, oh, man! What the hell was it all about? Maybe I got hold of some bad dope. I was used to drug cocktails. I often mixed my drugs, but this was too much even for me. It could have been a flashback to a bad acid trip, but I never had a trip like that, even in prison. Never.

I checked myself over from stem to stern. My body was in one piece and I looked the same and seemed to be able to function normally.

Well, there had been no physical manifestation of my experience. It had obviously all been in my head. I had lost my mind for two days—or did I?

Scared, I actually started to refuse drugs. Not all the time, but most of the time. I didn't go on scores anymore.

Still, my daily routine didn't change much. Everyday, I would walk around as usual and meet up with the gang around 3:00 P.M. at the bar. That was social time: the drug dealers taking a break between deals; the daytime hookers finished for the day or also taking a break; and the boosters with bags full of swag that could be moved within the hour to the bartenders, waiters, bouncers and regular customers. They were all there, but only the inner circle sat at the big table.

I was still one of the inner circle, I told myself, and sat with them in the same chairs every day near the back door exit—just

155

in case. The backdoor of this bar, as well as those of many neighboring restaurants and gambling joints, led into an alley that Chinatown shared: the smells of rotten cabbage: the singsong dialects of Mandarin and Canton provinces: the old Chinese men shuffling along and the young bucks swaggering: the Chinese women who were the foundation on which everything was built.

I knew Chinatown long before it was a gleam in Jack Nicholson's eye.

CHAPTER TEN

Chinatown

Vancouver's Chinatown had started to strain at the seams. Immigration quotas had been relaxed, and now there were little or no restrictions on the Asians allowed immigration. While many of the new immigrants were good, hardworking individuals being afforded the opportunity for a new and more prosperous life, it was the bad and the ugly behind them who would eventually attract the attention of law enforcement.

With the immigration gates opened wide, the slick, streetwise Hong Kong gangs came like a flood, drowning the good works of the hardworking Chinese. Of course, it wasn't like there had never been criminals in Chinatown. Now, there were just more of them.

All heroin that came into Vancouver was touched by a Chinese hand at some point, but because of the many secret societies that operated within Chinatown, the police had a hard time tracking the families down. There would be busts, but only when the heroin had passed on to the Gwailos, or Caucasians. Whites from the West End depended on the Chinese for their supply of heroin, but unlike the Chinese, they didn't know how to handle secrecy, so that was the arena the police concentrated on patrolling.

Cocaine was not our target drug here. Opium and its more refined sister, heroin, were. Actually, any principal alkaloid of opium was considered a good bust for God and country. We had bought a great deal of opium and heroin, pounds of it, and we had clean cases for the courts before our first cocaine buy.

At that time, cocaine was making a very big entrance on the competitive drug stage. The players started to take the drug for recreation until they were made aware of the money that could be made from dealing the stuff. Anyone with the money could get into the coke business. Unlike opium and heroin, coke was an open market.

Cocaine came into Canada by the boat load, and it had already hit the white middle to upper classes. Lawyers, especially, were weak for it. Cocaine was easy to peddle, too, because it offered a sexual promise that they could not refuse. Women liked the lifestyle of the men who took it. It meant that there was money, and when the men were under the influence of the powder, they were always very generous.

The professional businesspeople believed that cocaine was a "clean" drug, not "dirty" like heroin. Little did they know that cocaine did more to support organized crime than any other illegal activity. Heroin, in contrast, targeted the down and out. People who had reached the bottom of the food chain. Unless heroin was forced upon a person, the user was probably a misfit in a life that had been so hard on him or her that the only thing left was to give in to Morpheus.

Cocaine, on the other hand, targeted the up and coming elite. That knowledge gave the pusher power he never had before. He was now a welcome guest in homes that had been off limits to his sort of scum only a few years before. Suddenly, the cocaine pusher became respectable overnight.

Bankers, lawyers, judges, brokers, police officers, just to name a few, now mixed with the street person. Cocaine was the equalizer that brought us all together. Yes, even the street girl gone good and the RCMPs gone bad. We were all in it together.

The police had long ago decided that it was a waste of time and money to concentrate on the Chinese directly. Sometimes, it would take up to ten years of around-the-clock surveillance just to arrest a big man in the drug trade—and make it stick. The problem was, the police had no one, absolutely no one, who could successfully infiltrate Chinatown.

On the surface, though, Chinatown was a bustling, colorful and happy place. Restaurants catering to Western tastes were being replaced by traditional cuisine because of the demand driven by new immigrants who wanted to stay as close to their roots as possible. These new immigrants spoke dialects that had never before been heard in Chinatown. Cantonese and Mandarin were being rapidly replaced by Swatonese, Chiu Chao and Szechuan.

As for entertainment, Chinese movie houses sprang up everywhere. So did nightclubs that exclusively featured Chinese entertainers.

Diversity proved to be good for business. Real estate boomed because of the rich Hong Kong Chinese. Street hawkers spruced up their vending carts. Construction in Chinatown put a new face on some ancient buildings. And the night came alive with the vibrant faces and thick wallets of the young, the rich and the powerful.

Not all looked upon this newfound prosperity as a boon, however. The older Chinese were astounded by the militant mindset of the newcomers. These new people represented a China and Hong Kong that was alien to them.

I, Mah May Wan, was a witness to history here as I had been in New York. It must have seemed remarkable to the non-Chinese visiting Chinatown to see me coming and going, interacting with the community and her people as an equal, accepted in places that were off limits to outsiders, even doorways that lead to gambling halls and private, backroom tea shops. The private men's clubs had guards posted like bouncers—only more deadly. They stood in the doorways all up and down the streets of Chinatown, but I went in whenever and wherever I wanted to go. No one stopped me.

Looking at me, no one would doubt that I could pass for half-Chinese, but armed with the knowledge of the culture and my bold attitude, it was no problem. Chinese woman tend to be slender, so I lost some weight. I very rarely wore high heels. I did use heavy eye makeup to give me an exotic look. I changed my voice and accent depending on what group of Chinese I was in.

For example, Hakka women are very loud, but Mandarin women are soft-spoken.

As I moved mostly among men and was not a full-blooded Chinese, it was understood that I would have some rough edges.

One afternoon, I went to Tang's restaurant and, after getting myself a cup of tea, walked over to the the oldest, most bent-over man there was. He was dressed in unmatched baggy trousers and a worn blue jacket. His tie had a hundred dinners on it and he was toothless. An old man of eighty or ninety or a hundred, who knew?

"How are you today, uncle," I said in the Toishan dialect, and kissed the top of his head. Not waiting for an answer, I sat down beside him, and we drank our tea in respectful silence. When I finished, I washed my cup out, put it away and walk outside.

"Who was that kindly old man?" I asked a familiar face who had wandered outside and was now standing beside me.

"He is the head man of the Triad organization that has been operating out of Vancouver and Seattle for many years. Didn't you know that?" she said.

I shook my head no.

Well, the police never found out who he was, so I didn't feel too bad.

The old school of Chinese didn't flaunt their wealth. Every day was the same. Dress modestly, act modestly, eat modestly. Tea and dim sum, noodles, duck, simple foods . . . the list goes on and on. The young ones, of course, are different now as then. Arrogant and flashy in their silk Hong Kong suits and designer haircuts, driving BMWs.

I took a deep vreath and began walking. My mixed-up thoughts about my mixed-up life traveled along with me. I must have looked preoccupied, or worse. One of the cops working in the area stopped me and asked how I was.

Street people interacted with the beat cops daily. We knew their names. Good cops treated us like human beings. They would stop and ask us how we were doing. If we were obviously out of control from drugs, they would send us home or walk us to the police station only two or three blocks away from the district, and let us sleep it off in the drunk tank. It was usually done for our own safety.

Oh, there were one or two mean ones. When we saw them coming, we scattered. These were the dirty cops with super egos. They were into rousting sick junkies with sticks and threats. That made them big in law enforcement, among the cops who didn't know any better. But we knew better. They were as sick as the poor winos and druggies they tortured. I knew them all.

During my daily observations, I learned their names. Some were city cops, others were with the Federal police force, the same RCMP that had carted me off to prison years before.

Even in those days, I had a natural talent for getting information from people without tipping my hand. The name Stan Dumanski was dropped a lot. The word on the street was he was fair and didn't rough people up without provocation, as most narco cops did back then—and still do. Stan was more concerned with getting "the man," not some poor street junkie.

Day in and day out, I now wandered the streets. Something inside me would not let me rest, was propelling me forward, toward what I didn't yet know.

The summer was almost over. The days were still sunny and warm, but there was an undercurrent of crispness in the air.

One day, I started talking to a narc who'd befriended me, Ty Eschelmann.

"Supposing somebody wanted to turn," I said, smoking a cigarette.

"Uh-huh," Ty answered, his ruddy cheeks puffing out with the smoke.

"Now suppose that person could be valuable."

"You mean, like an informer?"

"No. No way," I responded vehemently. Informers were pariahs who, for ten pieces of silver, turned on their own. They had no morals and no ethics.

"I might be interested in someone like that. But not you, eh?"

"Of course, not me," I replied and then quickly walked away.

A few weeks went by and Ty had me meet with his partner, Didier DuMont.

"I hear you want to help us out."

"I didn't say that."

"Well, I hear you're interested in working with us."

"Maybe."

We talked a bit longer and I filled him in on some of my criminal history. That night, the phone rang in the flop house where I had a room. It was the RCMP officer I'd heard so much about.

"My name's Stan Dumanski. I hear we might have interests in common. Why don't we get together and talk?"

"You buying?"

He laughed.

"As long as it's not lobster. My company doesn't have such a large budget."

We met in an out of the way Italian restaurant on a sidestreet in one of the more deserted sections of the city. Ty and Didier were already there when I got there. They escorted me to a booth where a man was already sitting.

"Dorothy, meet Stan Dumanski," said Ty.

A big bear of a man well over 6'2" and 200 pounds, Stan stood up and shook my hand with a paw the size of a baseball glove.

"Great to meet you," he said with genuine warmth. "Please sit down."

I sat in the booth, Ty beside me and Didier next to Stan.

"I've heard a lot about you," Stan said.

I said nothing, and Stan took a notebook out of the inside pocket of his sports jacket. He paged through his notes.

"Uh, let's see, yeah. Convicted of kidnapping and armed robbery at age sixteen. Escaped from Kingston Prison."

"Twice," I said defiantly.

Stan smiled back. "Of course, twice. I always give credit where credit is due."

"And let's see, uh, assorted felonies and misdemeanors when you were a kid."

He looked up from the notebook.

"Kind of precocious, huh?"

"Kind of." I swallowed hard.

"Okay, look," I began. "Here's the dope and it's all true. Check it out. I was a drug dealer for years. I worked with Richard Wheeler—"

"Cadillac Richie?" Didier interrupted.

"That's right. And Richard Hill and Nikki Barnes. I've run scams in every city in Canada and more than a few in the States as well as in other countries."

"And I hear you have contacts in Chinatown," Stan said slowly.

"I don't talk about it, but take my word. I'm at home in every Chinatown in the world. I have contacts with the Triad—"

"The Triad?" Stan repeated.

"That's right, contacts with the Triad."

"Including here in Vancouver?" Ty asked.

"Here in Vancouver too," I assured him.

"Why don't you excuse us, now, will you boys?" Stan asked. Didier and Ty reluctantly left.

163

"Look, Dorothy—"

"Wan. My Chinese name is Mah May Wan and that's the name I'm currently using."

Stan smiled, almost paternally. "Tell me something. How have you managed to be a criminal so long but the only time you were caught was when you were a kid?"

"Well, being a kid was part of it. I got smarter as I got older and I used my talents to mimic people, to dress in different costumes—"

"I've heard about your disguises," he said, watching me closely.

I nodded. "I guess I take on the characteristics of whatever community I'm in, including dress, manner, whatever—the whole package."

"You're sort of like a chameleon, aren't you?"

"Exactly."

Stan thought for a moment, then leaned toward me.

"Look, Wan. Have you ever thought of using that talent on the right side of the law?"

"How do you mean?"

"Utilizing your criminal background and your ability to disguise yourself and blend in. I bet the chameleon part is your real talent. I want you to think about doing something positive with it instead of destroying yourself and others."

He got up to go.

"Hey Stan."

He turned.

"This new career. What do you call it?"

"Crown agent," he said and, followed by Didier and Ty, he walked out.

"I like it," I said half to myself. "Crown agent."

Within days, I called Stan and said yes.

After that, Stan took me under his wing. I began thinking differently about myself. My life had changed. I had changed. My lifestyle had not.

I was on the street everyday, mixing with all the same people, keeping the same hours. Most of the time, I was a loner, so no one was suspicious of me not getting involved in their action. I still had money every day in my leather jacket, only this time it was my government's money.

This way, I was always able to hold my own and pay my own way. That was necessary to maintain my cover. The only difference was, I was mentally recording everything that was being said; things that I had not paid attention to before now became very important—dates, time, ports of entry and names.

I had all the skills necessary to do the job, plus the added twist that the street people totally accepted me. Moreover, I had promised myself I would do it right. The RCMP had an honest, loyal agent, one who was not playing both sides of the fence. One who was not an informer.

During the next few months, Stan and I had many talks, acquainting me with the way things worked. "Your job is to be an undercover civilian agent," he said, "to go in and establish who the criminals are."

"And then?" I asked.

"And then, once you're firmly established, you introduce your partner, who'll be an undercover cop. He'll make the buys and arrange for the busts. It's easier that way in court, because the undercover's testimony will be believed absolutely, while yours might not be."

Stan was nothing if not diplomatic.

A few days later, I saw some fat cat putting the boots to a sick junkie. I walked closer. The junkie was Frankie, the woman that had been in prison with me and called me "nigger." She was now about forty-five years-old, down and out. No more Miss Big Shot. Frankie's hair had gone thin and dirty, her skin grey, she had some missing teeth and the ones remaining were black with decay.

"Come on Gene, gimme my fix," she begged her dealer.

The rules are, junkies do not approach the man in public. They are only to talk to the runners. A dealer doesn't even want to be in the same room with a "hype."

Frankie was obviously so desperate, the rules didn't matter to her. After all, I later found out, in the old days she and Gene made some big money together. But now she was a customer and one without money, the necessary commodity.

"Gene, I'm short cash," she pleaded. In other words, she didn't have enough money to buy a fix.

"Come one, you'll help me out, right?"

That's not how it works on the street. I had learned it the first day I got to New York.

I watched Frankie writhing on the ground, Gene's boots catching her in the stomach and chest. If I interfered, I'd blow my cover, but as I walked past, I became a woman with a mission.

Frankie and I made eye contact. She was the baby stuck in the mud, hands reaching up towards me. Crossing the street, Frankie's words came back to me.

"Niggers can dance," she'd said.

Well Frankie, I thought, maybe you'll never see me dance, but when this dealer goes down, I'll be dancing just for you baby.

A month later, another person put their boot on Frankie's chest, only this one used it to turn her over onto her back. Lifeless eyes stared back up at him. Frankie was dead from an overdose.

I mourn Frankie to this day. There but for the grace of God . . .

After her death, I became committed to a singular mission. I was now ready to stop the hemorrhaging of life, the killing. I was ready to do more, to be part of a team.

I hit the streets, doing some easy jobs at first. I went into bars, hung around, established who the local dealers were and then reported back to Stan with the information. This was low- level, street stuff. Stan just wanted to establish that I could do the job.

When he felt sure I was ready, Stan told me the real reason he'd recruited me.

"We've been wanting for years to go after the Triad, but they always make our undercovers. With your experience, though, you're in; we got a shot at busting some heavy dudes."

It would take courage and be quite dangerous. Among the world's criminal enterprises, the Triad was probably the oldest, and perhaps, the deadliest.

But I knew I would do quite well. Most undercover cops are so busy trying to keep the street from touching them, they appear out of place while on assignments. Even when dealing with upper level dealers, they sometimes want to act superior. But the only one way to work effectively undercover is to tap into the rhythm of the street.

You gotta be able to sit on those dirty chairs and use the dirty bathrooms and eat and drink in dives without showing offense. My home had always been the streets, but now I'd crossed over to the other side.

There was a long way to go, but finally, I was a good guy.

CHAPTER ELEVEN

The Triad

I had lived among and within the Chinese community all my life. Every city across Canada had a Chinese community where I had contacts. Even if it was a small town with one Chinese family, I'd have a nodding acquaintance with them based on a secret, shared bond. And because we existed on the same plane, in such an intimate manner, Stan knew I was the perfect choice to infiltrate the Triad and cripple their drug operation, because I was already totally accepted by them before the operation began.

By Triad, I mean *the* Triad, not the copycat gangs out there calling themselves "Triad." It's almost like the young Italian punks who call themselves the Mafia because they figure they've seen "The Godfather" ten times and know how to act and sound like Marlon Brando.

Sure, some Chinese gangs are dangerous, but they are nothing more than unruly outlaws. In contrast, the Triad is very much in control. They are so incredibly big, they're untouchable. A blink, a wink, a nod or even a subtle hand gesture could cause a ripple to be felt in businesses all over the world—and the source would never be known.

Traditionally, in centuries past, the Triad movement in China was a low-profile crime organization consisting of only family members. Individual members were quickly drummed out of the clan if they sought the spotlight.

As the families grew, branches were formed and a pecking order of rank was put into place. They were a law unto themselves.

Historically, Triad infighting was so serious and violent that many times, the movement went to the verge of extinction. Even today, there are few assassinations outside the group, but many within. In fact, the Triads kill within their families for the slightest infraction but take great pains and consideration before giving the order to kill outside their society. They lean towards resolving problems peacefully in order to remain safe. This is their main concern, of course. No suspicion is to be directed towards them.

The ultimate success of this ancient organization depends upon total loyalty. Originally, it was agreed that one person, "President for Life," had to be installed. An oath was sworn to obey at all times any orders given by this individual. The punishment for any member breaking this oath was, and is, a horrible death.

As years passed, members were encouraged to educate themselves and become knowledgeable in all things. They became Renaissance men and women, moving freely among high society. No community was off limits to them: science, politics, the arts, etc. They would systematically and strategically infiltrate these areas and combine their legitimate training with their dark side and sabotage, rebuild and redirect whatever they were into, thereby benefiting the Triad movement. Today, the Triads have infiltrated every facet of modern society.

In Vancouver, Toronto, Montreal and Calgary, as well as stateside in New York, San Francisco and Europe, Triad organizations including the Kung Lok Society, the 14K, the Wah Ching, the Gum Wah and the Lotus Society, mix ancestral worship and superstition with modern day trappings to keep the Triad members in line. While it is hard to estimate active Triad membership in other countries, in Hong Kong, where many

Triads have their roots, the Royal Hong Kong Police Force estimates between 70,000 to 120,000 active, part-time and inactive members. Their numbers, though, are disproportionate to their power. However, in China and occidental countries with Chinese neighborhoods, the police are often on the Triad payroll, and even Triad members themselves. Also, high government officials in China are Triad members—or sleeping with them.

Understand that these people do not see themselves as dirty or corrupt. The contemporary profile of a Triad member is a sophisticated, well-dressed lady or gentleman who is accommodating, subservient to those in power, family-oriented, highly moral, supportive of their community, quiet in demeanor and evasive of the limelight.

They are honor-bound by the code of ethics and laws laid down by their ancestors centuries ago. It is their duty to obey, thereby respecting the culture and traditions of a people who claim to be the most ancient on earth.

Police had made some inroads over the years into the Chinese drug trade, a bust here, a bust there, but nothing substantial. The big problem was that the law-abiding Chinese would not cooperate with the police because even they owed a loyalty to the Triad, often for a favor from long ago.

That favor might have involved paying the passage of a loved one to safety years ago, or settling a family feud in such a way that everyone saved face. It could be anything from arranging a marriage to paying a gambling debt. Whatever the favor was, it was understood that the family so helped would always be loyal from generation to generation. This concept is taught Chinese children from childhood.

It is also understood that the Triad need not call in their markers for three or more generations. At such time, a family that was helped in 1920 would be asked to make good on the debt in 1995. It is an elegant conceit—do a favor in one generation and enslave lifetimes of future ones.

Many Chinese, both in their native country and in their adopted ones, come from large families. Those in China are the most poor and need their successful relatives in the West to help them. The Triad can stop the mail to these poor relatives in China's remote villages, and because the mail may contain food and, more importantly money, it really is a matter of life and death that the connection be maintained.

The substance that has been used to maintain that connection is one linked to the Chinese people forever—opium. Since the plant has to be cultivated, it is the hill chiefs who still wield the most power as it is they who are the link between those who have the drug and those who want it.

The true story of the Triad may never be told, although many a scholar seem to think they've gotten it simply because some Triad member or high-ranking Hong Kong police official discussed Triad business with them. Little do these would-be detectives know that there is but one account, true in some detail but false in substance, given to the outside world. The real, true history has been kept secret, jealously guarded for centuries.

As for the cops, where do they get their facts? From crooks and people from the street. Not surprisingly, their so-called facts are usually not facts at all.

Yet the world's police forces, particularly in the United States and Canada, continue to chase the proverbial rabbit while the Triad stays well-hidden in the pack for another thousand years. The Triad takes much delight in planting the seeds of deception into the Western mind.

One rainy night, I was in Long's, a popular Chinese nightclub. It was located on the edge of Chinatown. A seedy residential neighborhood bounded it on the other side. The residents had long since stopped painting their homes or cultivating their lawns.

Stairs from the street went straight up to the third floor, where the club was. A round-faced doorman of indeterminate age sat at the top to keep an eye peeled, more for the cops than to keep the peace. He would switch the lights if the cops even looked up the stairs.

Only the very heavy players frequented the place. It was owned and operated by the Long Family (husband and wife). Now the name Long is about as common as the name Smith. However, these Longs operated the kind of place where whiskey was served in a tea pot with the special dish of the day.

The lighting was very dim, not unlike some of the places in the Harlem of my youth, but deadlier. Long's was not a place where you went if there were people looking to hurt you, because a person could be dead in his chair all night without anyone knowing. Poison, gunshot, a knifing, any kind of death could go down and no one would know. With all the noise from the floor show, loud talking and darkness, the waitress wouldn't bother a table unless a glass was empty.

You had to be sure of yourself and your enemies before hanging around Long's, and I was. We all had something else in common: drugs.

Long's was a drug supermarket. Many an international deal was put together in that bar on the corner of Fontaine Avenue and High Streets.

Coke was openly sniffed at the tables with just a glance towards the door, in case the cops decided they needed a bust to look good. But cops avoided the place like the plague. It was a bitch to take somebody out of that bar if they didn't want to go.

Along with a table full of regulars, I was sitting with an older Chinese man, an opium smuggler who was trying to move over a million dollars worth of counterfeit American currency.

"See if you can tell which is the real stuff," he said to us. We tried to identify the genuine the dollars which are also on the table, from the counterfeit bills. We had little success despite the fact that American money was very common in Vancouver.

Most of the drug business between the Chinese was in fact transacted in American money.

Another round of drinks was ordered, which was paid for with a bad one hundred dollar bill. Who cared if we passed it on to Mr. Long? He'd just move it around his business. He wouldn't take a loss. Nobody would suffer. We all laughed like hell as my eyes darted down surreptitiously to the serial numbers on the bills. We hadn't finished laughing at our little joke when one of the chorus girls came over to the table and whispered in my ear.

"There's some weird guy over there who's trying to buy a pound of heroin."

What square would act like that? Come into a strange bar and order a load from a customer that he'd never met before in his life.

"He's got a roll on him," the waitress purred into my ear.

Sounded interesting. Wonder how much he was prepared to spend?

When I walked over to his table, I tried my best not to laugh in his face. He was a baby-faced boy who looked like he'd just fallen off the turnip truck. He had a grin from ear to ear and was dressed like he didn't belong anywhere. He stuck out like a sore thumb. The guy had to be an undercover. Who else would look that stupid?

Still, I might be wrong. I knew of no other undercover operation in the vicinity. Maybe this guy was just some prep school idiot looking to make a quick buck by dealing to his friends.

"Hi, how are you. I hear you're looking," I said.

He stood up and shook my hand and held the chair out for me to sit down. Was he for real? Everyone in the bar was watching to see what I was going to do.

I sat down. I'd play the sucker until he showed his hand.

"What'll you have?"

"Scotch. A double."

The waitress came over and he ordered for me.

"Where you from?"

"Montreal," he answered proudly.

The drink came and I sipped it. They had given me the good stuff, Johnnie Walker Black, not the generic brand they gave to most of the customers.

"What are you doing in Vancouver?"

"I want to buy some heroin."

Just like that. I could hardly contain myself. No one says they want to buy heroin, even if you know each other.

First of all, if he was a real drug dealer, this would not be the approach. If he came from out-of-town with no connection, he would have eased himself into the action. Same thing applies for an undercover cop.

"So why are you asking me for heroin? I could be a cop and set you up."

He laughed and said, "You, you're no cop. I can smell a cop." I doubted his honker was that sensitive. Then I looked into his eyes. They scared the hell out of me.

One was green and one was brown, or was it the light? I couldn't let him know that his eyes shook me. I kept a steady stare, no smile and said, "If I'm not a cop, than who is?"

"Not me lady. I'm a drug dealer from Montreal. All I want is a pound of heroin."

I started to laugh, tried to stifle it, and finally just let it go. I just kept on, until tears were running down my face.

"Who the fuck are you?" I finally asked.

I burst out laughing again.

"My name is Josh," he said seriously.

"Well, Josh, do you do blow?"

"Blow?"

"Yes, blow, coke, sniff, uno uno, girl, lines?"

"What?"

"Cocaine, you stupid fuck!" I said with exasperation.

"Oh, yes, please."

"Yes, please," I repeated with more than a trace of sarcasm.

Boy, I was getting tired with this guy. I didn't know who was trying to pull whose chain.

"I have money. Can I buy some cocaine?" he asked after thinking about it for a second. I nodded.

"Okay, let's you and me go get a few grams."

I did not want to buy any in the bar. The guy was worrying me, so I wanted to get out of there fast.

What should I do? Burn him or save him? I didn't know. He didn't even have a car, so I went to the front of the club where two guys I knew were sitting. They had just come in and had not seen me or my new "friend."

"Could you guys give me a ride to Big's to get some blow?"

"Sure," they answered. "We just gave a guy a ride there and back downtown an hour ago. The cheap bastard didn't even give us a line."

"Look, I'll pay for the gas and buy you a drink when we get back but I can't promise you any dope. It's not my play."

They thought about that for a minute. "Okay," they said, "let's go."

I went to get Josh.

"Holy shit," said the two shitheads. "It's the same guy we drove to Big Mama's."

They didn't want to go again. They smelled a rat. I took them aside.

"Look, the dude's new in town and just checking things out."

They looked at him. Josh just stood there with that stupid grin on his face. I managed to talk them out of being suspicious. Before they had a chance to change their minds, I grabbed his arm and we all left.

Josh gave them money for the coke and a little extra. When we got to Big Mama's, the car was parked in the back alley. We stayed in the car with one of the guys while the other went inside and made the deal. I wanted to go back to the club but not Josh.

"I need to go to my hotel," he said, after getting the drugs. He was suddenly assertive. "I'll take a cab." It sounded like an excuse but I saw no reason to talk him out of it.

We drove him to a busy street so he could flag his taxi. Before he got out, I asked him where I could reach him so that we could talk more about our earlier conversation. Anxious to talk to me again, he gave me his hotel and room number.

Josh had given me a lot of information during our conversations and if he was telling me the truth, he could be checked out easily enough. Stan and the boys would see to that. I had to meet them after Long's closed, when I'd run it by them.

Back at the club, I finished off the night, spending most of my time thinking. I had already made up my mind that Josh was a cop, a dumb cop—what's new?—but a cop never-the-less.

In the empty hours of the morning, I met Stan and Didier and they debriefed me. A debriefing is when you just repeat what you've seen and heard and answer any questions they might have.

As the sun was peeking over the horizon, and the debriefing was ending, I got a strange feeling. Stan was pretty organized; he always knew what was happening. Which meant . . .

"Listen, Stan, you've got to pull that undercover dude off the streets before he gets himself killed. Or, just keep him away from me," I warned.

They played the game with me, not wanting me to know that I had made their man, but I could tell by their lack of eye contact and stiff body movements.

"No, we don't know an undercover named Josh," Stan lied. "Do you, Didier?"

"No, me either." Didier was a better liar. He actually looked me straight in the eye. But they stiffened when I gave them his hotel and room numbers.

See, Josh had made a mistake the size of the Empire State Building. If an undercover is not set up by his department with an apartment or house, whatever the project called for, he is not supposed to give his location to people. He was probably just in time for a tryout and blew it, big time. I knew I had hit it right.

Two weeks later, Stan said during one of our debriefings, "Okay, you were right about that guy."

"What guy?"

Stan smiled.

"You know who I'm talking about."

"Oh, Josh, yeah."

"He's one of ours," Stan admitted. "And we need your help with him. How would you like your first partner?"

I felt like walking away, but reluctantly, I agreed.

I learned the rest of the story after two weeks of playing nurse-maid to Josh, whose full name was Joshua LaForge. The RCMP had to decide what to do with him. Should they send him back to Montreal or give him to me to train in the ways of the street?

There were many problems with this situation. The English Canadians had a hard time working with the French Canadians, a conflict that's still a problem in the RCMP today. Now me, I didn't have a problem with the French. How could I?

I was neither entirely English nor fully French Canadian. I was a mongrel. Also, I had spent many hours with French Canadian people and they had always been wonderful to me. However, French Canadian police officers were somewhat different from their English colleagues in their approach to law enforcement . Some adjustments were necessary, for sure.

If this project was going to get off the ground, we had to decide on an RCMP to work with me. If we didn't use Josh, we'd have to wait another month or so for another undercover to be available. In his defense, the big guy did have some things going for him.

His French accent would get him off the hook if he made a mistake in communicating with the Chinese. He had reddish-brown hair that he wore in an Afro—and those crazy, mismatched eyes. His tanned skin set off his good looks. Overall, his look was great.

178

Eventually, everyone agreed to keep Josh. I found out that Josh also had a mixed heritage and had been adopted by a French Canadian couple from a very small town near Montreal. His was a quiet background. That soon changed when he became a wild man for the RCMP.

Josh must have invented the term "party animal." After we taught him how to dress and put him in a Datsun sports car, he was on his way to the fast track. How he was allowed to get away with his drinking and drugging, I do not know.

He was rude and arrogant toward all of us.

One of the best busts we made involved two, big-time heroin traffickers, Ernie Young and Felix Li. Young had a furniture store on Burke Street, where we went to visit him. We wanted to talk turkey there but because there was somebody else in the store who none of us knew, we decided to go to Long's, where we could talk privately.

As we were walking, Josh said, "My friend told me that when I'm ready, I can come and see you."

"How much do you want?" Ernie replied, getting right down to business.

"It all depends on the price and the quality," Josh said, exactly like I'd taught him.

"It's grade three. It's not powder and it's twenty-three grand."

"How come the price is so low?" I wondered out loud.

"It's because we cut out themiddlemen," Ernie explained.

Now, grade three heroin is fairly high quality, commonly referred to among dealers and junkies as "red chicken," so I was surprised.

After we got to the restaurant, Ernie arranged for us to meet Felix Li the next day. Li was the supplier. The next day, the deal went down at Ernie's furniture store: a pound of heroin was exchanged for $23,000.

That was my first project. From the standpoint of the public, we did a bang-up job, but I knew we'd only made a small beginning. It was the top guys, the upper echelons of the drug culture, that I wanted to take down. The ones who were selling their poison on a million dollar basis and inflicting their poison on millions of citizens—they deserved to pay for their crimes.

During the next two years, I got my shot at the "big men." Josh and I took down some of the biggest Triad members in Canada, the United States, the United Kingdom and Hong Kong.

One of the most well-connected was Aaron Sung. Aaron was a rare bird. Not only was he a full-blooded Chinese, born and raised on the streets of Vancouver and Seattle, but he had completely immersed himself in North American culture. He got this way right down to the nasty habit of leaving his first wife, who was native Chinese, and their children. He was about forty years old, silver-haired, taller than most Asians and very handsome. The women on Aaron's arm at the fancy restaurants and nightclubs were showpieces.

He'd become so firmly ensconced with non-Chinese society that the international Triad used, and even depended upon him to act as liaison between them and the "round eyes."

I knew Aaron for years before I became an agent, just as I had known many of the others who were to become my targets. When the RCMP singled him out, I was able to introduce him to Josh without a problem.

At first, our transactions with Aaron were small, but within a couple of weeks we put together a seven figure deal for some China White.

"I'm going to use my nephew, Bruce, and his wife Lily to middle the deal," Aaron said.

"How do we know he's all right?" Josh asked before I could stop him. Aaron shot him a withering look.

"You know because I say it," he said in an emotionless voice.

A time and place were set for three days later, twelve noon, in the city park. The Chinese do much of their drug business during the daytime. The more traffic, the more people, the more camouflage, the better.

This day turned out to be a scorcher. Josh sat in our car, which was thankfully parked under a shade maple in full foliage. I got out and made my way through the park entrance and walked around aimlessly.

"Hello, Mah." I turned to see a pleasant-looking young man with thick black hair and horn-rimmed glasses coming up behind me.

"I'm Bruce Sung."

On a half-hidden, rusty bench, I unobtrusively tested the product while we shared some ice tea. Then, we agreed on the time and place for the pick up. When I was satisfied,, I paid him half the money in good faith, as we'd agreed with Aaron, and sauntered back to the car.

"What took you so long?" Josh demanded. "I could have done it in half the time."

"Sure you could," I shot back, "but would you know what you were doing and getting?"

I changed the subject and told him where and how we were going to make the pick up

"Bruce and his wife and baby are going out to lunch tomorrow at Marco Polo's. We'll meet them there and make the exchange," I said, explaining the rest.

At noon the next day, Josh and I were already sitting at the table in the restaurant when Bruce and Lily appeared, wheeling their baby in a stroller. Lily kissed each of us on the cheek.

"So glad you could both come," she said pleasantly.

"Tricia looks so cute in her new blue dress," I said. Jessica beamed.

"It's the one you got her."

Nice touch, I thought.

"Would you like to come to they ladies room with me while I change her?"

I nodded. Damn right, I would. The China White was in the baby's diaper.

Bruce and Josh sat at the table looking out for trouble.

Lily and I strolled to the bathroom, went inside and busied ourselves with the baby, waiting for the bathroom to be empty. Then, in a flash, we made the pass.

We ate our lunch in a leisurely fashion, and parted amicably.

"See you again soon," Bruce said when it was time to leave.

"Sooner than you think," I said under my breath, thinking of our future court date. We bid them good-bye.

A few hours later, we passed the stuff to the RCMP. The next morning, they arrested Aaron Sung.

David eventually gave us about five major players in the United States and Canada. He also gave us the details on many drug corridors, new ones that law enforcement officials could now close down.

These articles in the local paper were typical of the coverage our Triad busts got:

The Vancouver Sun

Mountie Tells of Arranging Drug Buy

A young RCMP undercover officer who posed as a big-time drug trafficker from Montreal told an Assize Court jury Tuesday that he arranged to purchase heroin from two Vancouver men for $23,000 a pound.

But in his guise as a big-time dealer, Constable Joshua LaForge said he never touched the heroin, choosing instead to have another incognito RCMP officer act as a "courier."

LaForge, 23, was testifying during the first day of the trial of Yuan (Ernie) Young, 24, and Felix Li, 35, who are charged with trafficking in heroin.

Another article read:

Judge Praises RCMP for Trafficker Roundup

Members of the RCMP Vancouver drug squad today were lauded for their "great skill and courage" in fighting drug trafficking.

The tribute to the Mounties was made by Mr. Justice P. Gregory Cleese at the close of a special Assize Court hearing into a series of drug trafficking offenses.

Mr. Justice Cleese recalled that the special assize was convened on Jan. 20 to deal with a series of direct indictments laid by the attorney-general of Canada.

During the assize, 17 defendants charged with trafficking in heroin, cocaine and opium received jailsentences ranging up to 215 years. The judge noted that the indictments arose out of RCMP undercover operations conducted in Vancouver last summer. He said Sgt. Stan Dumanski was in charge of the operation, which consisted of two undercover officers, Constables Josh LaForge and Zack Joliet, and six other men.

Of course, none of the articles could mention my name.

CHAPTER TWELVE

Ends and Beginnings

"Well Dorothy, the Triad investigation is over," Stan said. "Might be a good idea for you to get as far away from Vancouver as possible."

"I pissed them off, huh?"

Stan chuckled. "A little bit more than that. They put a contract out on you."

I felt honored. I'd done such a good job that they wanted me dead. I took a strange pride in that dubious honor. But then again, there was my safety to consider.

"So where do you want to go? Government pays all transportation and relocation expenses."

I knew how dogged the Triad could be in bringing their quarry to ground. Stan was right. As far away as possible would do the trick.

"Halifax," I told him. "I'll go back to my home province."

Halifax, located on the Atlantic coast, is the capital city of Nova Scotia.

"You're sure?"

"I'm sure," I assured him.

And then I was winging across country on the law's tab. The RCMP flew me back a couple of times to Vancouver to testify at the trials of the Triad big boys. I guess I didn't endear myself to them by doing this.

"That's just about it," Stan said in the closing days of the final trial. "Looks like we won't need you any more. Just make sure that wherever you are, you keep our people informed of your whereabouts just in case we need you for anything."

Well, that was the deal. A one shot deal. Stan had busted the people who had eluded him for a very long time. Now it was over. Stan had no more work for me. I left Vancouver despondent, feeling my days as a crown agent were short-lived and over.

Back in Halifax, I spent my time walking and thinking. The wind came off the water with a sharp bite to it. I passed the cemetery where many of the dead from the Titanic were buried. At least I'm better off than they are, I thought.

I enrolled in beauty school but found I couldn't cut it because of my lack of formal schooling and poor study skills. I dropped out. Time to hit the road again. Off I went to Ottawa. I had been there before when I'd hitched across the country and liked it. At that time, I had become friendly with some of the members of the Kaya crime family. They were into extortion, murder and drugs. But that was before, in my previous life.

I wondered what Ottawa held for me now.

My new name was Dorothy Hoffman, courtesy of the RCMP. They provided me with a different age and birthplace, complete with supporting legal documents.

As instructed, I notified the RCMP when I arrived in town. "We want you to meet with Corporal Paul VanDyck. He'll be your liaison, " I was told over the phone.

Tall, dark and handsome, Paul VanDyck looked like a recruiting poster for the Mounties. He was soft-spoken, well-groomed and seemed like a very nice guy.

Since I knew nothing about managing my finances, I had not yet had my money transferred from my bank in Halifax to a bank in Ottawa. Hell, this was the first time I had any business with a bank I wasn't thinking about robbing. From my adventures in the legal system, I knew it was a good idea to be represented, so I hired a lawyer to take care of the details for me.

"How you doing for cash?" Paul asked me over lunch.

"Well, I didn't ration my travel money very well. Until my money arrives from Halifax, I may have to go on welfare for some short-term help. Shouldn't be longer than a week."

His eyes examined me over the rim of his coffee cup.

"Here, Dorothy," Paul said, and put two hundred dollar bills in my hand. "That should hold you over."

I thought he was just some nice guy loaning me money. Then he came around every day the following week.

"I don't know why you can't show some appreciation to me. After all, I loaned you the money, didn't I?" Paul kept reminding me.

Guilt. That's a powerful emotion when you don't know how you're being manipulated, and you don't know how to take care of yourself. So I went to bed with him and in my mind, the debt was paid . . . in full. I was not going to pay twice.

"That bitch," he later told his boss. "She won't pay me back."

Someone who overheard the conversation told me about it. Of course, he left out the sexual extortion part. I never told his boss about it either. I was not going to embarrass myself in front of the brass. Still, I was determined not to cough up the money.

Paul hounded me, coming to my door at all hours of the day and night. The following week, I was washing dishes at a local restaurant. He came to the restaurant over and over and kept bothering me.

"Dorothy, we can't run a business this way," my boss told me.

I saw the writing on the wall. I quit before he fired me.

As if that wasn't enough, I began having trouble with the bank. The paperwork had gotten all mixed up. I was using two different names, one in Halifax, the other in Ottawa, and I forgot to change everything. To make matters worse, I owed my lawyer in Halifax, and he billed me. I sent a check to him, it bounced, and he called the RCMP in Ottawa, trying to find me.

Nothing was working out for me. Meanwhile, the Ottawa RCMP was angry.

"We're adding an unfavorable report to your file," Paul told me. His boss confirmed this.

I had all but given up when I got a surprise call from Chuck Terry, a Mountie who had talked with Stan.

"Listen Dorothy, we have some work for you. Interested?"

"Am I!" I answered, jumping at the chance to be a crown agent again.

We met at Naomi's, an out of the way restaurant.

"Here's the situation," said Chuck. "It's all very hush-hush. It seems some RCMP members are involved in some corrupt activity."

"Like what?"

"Welfare fraud and the like."

The job was pretty simple and they needed my help.

"We want you to infiltrate this group."

"Of corrupt cops."

"Right. We'll wire you. Get them to admit their wrongdoing."

"Then you and your boys— "

"Move in for the bust. Right."

It turned out to be an easy job. The dirty cops were more than willing to brag to a pretty girl how they'd ripped off the state.

There are no records or files about that project, no court appearances. It was handled internally. No mention of my involvement. I was paid cash as before, tax free, but I didn't have to sign any upfront agreement like before. I was told not to talk about it. I later found out that one of the Mounties that was under investigation, one of the guys I got the goods on, committed suicide.

I spent a short time in Ottawa. I did a few intelligence probes for the RCMP. I went into bars and social clubs, which were actually mob fronts, established myself as a player, and found out who the biggest drug dealers were, then I passed that information on to my bosses at "the Horse." It was in one such social club that I met Nicholas Pugliese.

Nicky had a record a mile long. Born into a mob family in Calabria, Italy, he'd immigrated to Canada where he quickly established himself as an up-coming criminal. He'd been in and

188

out of trouble with the law since he was a teenager. All kinds of rumors floated around about him. One of the most well known was that a cop had gotten shot some years back and Nicky had been fingered for it, but the police couldn't make it stick. He was also rumored to have shot men who crossed him. No witnesses to testify against him could ever be found.

"I understand from my friends that you have some experience as a runner."

We were talking over espresso and cognac at a private table.

"So?"

"Well, I might have a job for you."

"Running? What, in a marathon?"

Nicky laughed.

"Hey, you got balls."

"I beg your pardon?" I said demurely, and Nicky laughed again.

When I saw Nicky a couple of days later, he seemed to have forgotten about our conversation. Evidently, he had gotten someone to do the job he required. Nothing else happened and as I was restless, I moved to Calgary.

I wasn't too worried about the contracts the Triad had out on me. I was careful and I had the protection of knowing how the members think.

First of all, Felix Li and the other Triad members I'd helped put away were going to be behind bars for a long, long time. Anyone looking for me on their behalf would need to know what I looked like, and I changed my appearance from day to day.

One day, I would appear with my hair in a bun, the next straight back. Sometimes I wore heavy make-up, others none at all. Rouge under my cheeks made my cheekbones stand out. A dusting of the right powder could give me a prison pallor.

Bright dresses, drab dresses; pants and suits; dyke or call girl. It was all the same to me, anything to throw them off the scent. I was so good at changing my look that one day on the street I passed Joe Chin, a short, dark haired guy who I recognized from the Vancouver Triad. I looked straight at him— if I looked away that would attract attention— and he never recognized me. He had been one of the bad guys on the periphery, we saw each other regular for two years and still, he never knew it was me.

"Ya hear, Dorothy Hoffman's in town."

"Hoffman's in town. Yeah, the same broad who helped bust the Triad."

"Hoffman's good. Gets the job done."

These words passed through the Calgary headquarters of the RCMP. Soon, I was in demand by undercover teams. I had gotten a reputation.

"Dorothy, we want you to go into that players (criminals) bar downtown and see what you can find out."

"Dorothy, how about taking some time to work with us? We got a really interesting case involving some smuggling from the Bonnano family in New York contacts."

Among others, I took that one. And as the assignments warranted, I would change my appearance, my race, my ethnic group and go in after the targets.

The word spread.

"Dorothy Hoffman's good. She never goes after a target she can't take out."

Now I was given targets that police agents could not touch, not for lack of trying but because they just didn't have the ability to get close enough. They were called impossible targets. That's where I came in.

The impossible targets were given to me as a challenge. I accepted them. Of course, I could get close. I cut my baby teeth on those scumbags.

CHAPTER THIRTEEN

Internal Corruption

Once again, I was relocated, this time to Ottawa. I connected with my RCMP handlers, my field controllers, Corporals Albert Talman and Harry Minors, who sent me into the players bar, Le Bistro, to conduct an intelligence probe.

"A lot of drug dealers hang out in that place, Dorothy," Talman, told me. He was big and burly, unshaven most of the time and slovenly, like an overgrown country boy.

"Yeah, a lot of dealers hang out there," Minors echoed. "We want you to find out who's doing the selling so we can take them down."

Within the week I did my research. I was ready. I walked out of my apartment building at 2:00 A.M. on a moonless night dressed for bear wearing tight black pants that highlighted every contour of my legs, and black spiked heels. The jade green silk blouse billowed out at just the right places, helped a little by the underwire bra I had on underneath. I may have looked like a pro, but it didn't mean anything. I was just in my working clothes, same as a doctor who puts on a white coat or a stock broker wearing a three piece suit.

I'd just called a cab five minutes before and it was already waiting for me at the curb. I opened the door and stepped in. The front door, not the back. The front seat of a cab is where I always ride, out of habit.

When I'm working undercover, I pounce on every chance for information cab drivers are a well of news. Cabbies sit all day, mostly just listening, going all over the city, ferrying all kinds of people high and low. If you get in to the front, proving you're a regular person like them they're disarmed. They talk to me, like a fountain gushing forth. And Michael Singh Awalia was no exception.

He was the driver of the cab I'd just gotten entered. For a few minutes we just exchanged small talk, but I knew that Michael was sizing me up.

My very long, black hair and tinted skin made him curious regarding my ethnic background. As always, I didn't volunteer anything.

"You look like you might have some East Indian blood," he said.

I simply agreed, once again crossing the line into the unknown world that other people created for me. "My name is Sacha," I smiled.

I was on my way to Le Bistro, located in the Market, Ottawa's red light district. Being a cabbie, Michael knew all the hot spots. He was very surprised I was going to one of them. Despite my outfit, I must have looked like a "good girl."

He started to tell me about himself. Michael was an immigrant from India with a wife and two kids. He took special pains to point out that he was Sikh rather than Hindu.

"Here," he said, in accented English. "Take my business card and pager number. Call me when you're finished with whatever you're doing and I'll come take you home."

There'd been some articles in the paper about Sikhs being responsible for terrorist uprisings in India. Could Michael . . . ?

Well, you try not to judge a book by its cover. Still, something was wrong with this guy, but nothing I could put my finger on. Whatever it was, I knew before I got to my destination that Michael was somebody I'd have to follow up on.

By the time we arrived, it was 2:30 A.M. and Le Bistro was closed, except to preferred customers. Of course, I already knew this, courtesy of my research. I'd been there before and the bouncer, stationed like a rock hard Buddha on a stool outside, knew me. He smiled and pulled the door open.

The smoke and the noise hit me like a wall. The place was packed. Through the haze, I saw the men and women at the bar.

The women were young and beautiful and very high class. I knew a lot of them, and those I didn't, I could still identify. These women loved power, fine wine, French cuisine and the best coke in town. However sleazy their behavior, they insisted on opulent surroundings.

As always, they'd party here for a few more hours and then be driven home or to a hotel where the party would continue. Their pay would be good food, good drinks, good drugs and maybe an invitation to an embassy party or two.

Most of the girls were what they seemed—party girls—but you can bet there were a few plants, girls on the mob payroll who'd be debriefed tomorrow by their mob friends.

The men they were with were some of Canada's best known diplomats, sports celebrities, businessmen, politicians and gangsters. I noticed Robert Altwater at the bar. Tonight he was just one of the players, his arm encircling a whore's tiny waist. This is great, I thought. If only Robert's constituents could see him now, would they vote for him come election time?

But Robert wasn't just another Member of Parliament: he was a party leader.

Why politicians are attracted to bad guys is a subject open for debate and will always be. Myself, I would rather deal with an all-out gangster than a politician.

A gangster knows what and who he is. A politician is a victim to anything out there; he is a puppet trying to please everyone and during the search for self, becomes dangerous, a deer caught in the headlights of the fast life. They always seem to be catching up. Eventually, most of them are devoured by their own weaknesses, thereby becoming an attractive target for the Mafia, who are ready and willing to make a deal with them.

And here Robert was, with all the other debauchers who liked to hang around with the "bad" guys, who got some sort of perverse kick palling around with gangsters who'd cut your throat for a kilo of heroin. Which just happened to be the reason I was there. My job was to find out who was doing the selling and to take them down.

As always, I tried to eliminate the no-shows and narrow the probe down to people who are worth my time. Through conversation and observation, I found out who to talk to.

The target never sees me as a threat. I never come on to him. Actually, I made myself as unavailable as possible.

I tried to project the fact that I'm for hire, and I always let them know I was no a party whore. That way, the target realized right from the beginning I was a business woman there to make money.

I was usually never the one to mention drugs first. I mentioned jewelry instead.

I flashed the diamond ring and bracelet loaned for the occasion.

"That's a nice piece you're wearing. Buy it in Canada or did you have that ring (chain, or bracelet) made for you?"

As I talked to the people around me, they started to get comfortable. Sometimes they asked me to get them some hot pieces from my contacts. It's hot all right, straight from the street where I bought it. And when I sold it to them, I always got more than what it was worth.

See, I want the players to know I didn't need them. I could wine and dine them. They saw me as somebody they wanted to know, or at least as their equal.

As our relationship moved along, I would let them know I was in the market for furs and bonds. I made them believe that I would fence anything for a profit. That's how, gradually, the players drew me into their circle. It could take a few days or a few weeks.

Once I brought down the level of mistrust into a comfort zone, I was in. That's when I let them know I'm in a position to help them if they want to move large amounts of drugs. This time was no different.

"Hi, how are you?" said a gruff voice in French accented English.

I looked up from my drink. An oversized guy had taken the seat next to me at the bar and was undressing me with his eyes. As soon as he did that, I knew I had him.

This time, I carried protection, though not in my purse like most women. My friend ice pick was nestled comfortably against the small of my back, under my clothes and in the waistband of the pants. I never carried it in a purse; that can get separated from you quickly. Or searched.

I prefer an ice pick to a knife. A knife is harder to position. With a knife, you slash; an ice pick penetrates quicker and deeper.

As the guy talked to me further, he reached across the bar for his drink. His coat fell away from his waist for a moment and I saw the Saturday Night Special tucked into his waistband. He saw that I saw. I smiled, my bright Pepsodent smile. He liked that.

We talked for hours. He said his name was Jean St. Jacques, that he ran a janitorial service. Right. Sure. And every janitor carries a gun in his pants.

I didn't show much interest in St. Jacques that night, but I came back to Le Bistro time after time. St. Jacques kept hitting on me but I politely declined his advances, until I'd learned enough to know that he was a big-time heroin dealer.

Once I knew he was a legitimate target, we started going out. I casually let drop that I'd run a heroin lab, which was true, and gradually, he began to trust me. St. Jacques was supplying heroin to Connecticut, where the Bonanno crime family of New

York had their dealers distribute it. Not only did my bosses want St. Jacques taken down, but so did the F.B.I. and the D.E.A. And I was the one who could trigger the bust.

St. Jacques was not television's suave, debonair version of a drug dealer. At 6'4", and 250 pounds, he was a big bear of a man. He had a bad, ruddy complexion, weak, pale blue eyes that were distorted by coke bottle lenses inside black, horned rim frames. He also smelled terrible, but he did have one, redeeming trait: Jean St. Jacques was a gourmet. Food was his one true area of connoisseurship.

We talked business for several months. On each occasion he took me to gourmet restaurants. Most of the time, I dressed casually, save for one item: St. Jacques loved for me to wear "fuck me" shoes—high, strappy four inch heels. So before every "date," I'd paint my toenails a glorious shade of red and strap on the shoes that would guarantee St. Jacques a hard-on. Which was good. Because if he concentrated on sex—he wasn't getting anything, from me anyway—his perceptions would be clouded and that would give me a little extra edge in case he found out who I really was.

My cover story was that I was a dealer and a "mule," someone who transports drugs from city to city. The RCMP force had set up the pedigree for me, and when St. Jacques checked my contacts, they all checked out.

I was in. Established. A few weeks later, St. Jacques took the bait.

"I want you to run a factory for me and maybe make a few runs down to Connecticut," he said during a particularly lovely dinner at Le Monde, a French restaurant in Ottawa.

I had this guy, I had this guy. But I showed nothing. I lowered my cup and looked up slowly.

"I want to see what your operation looks like first," I said, with a calm that surprised even me. "I'll only work for a real professional operation."

St. Jacques laughed. "Fair enough. Tomorrow I'll take you to the cottage."

It was early spring, and the next day, though there was a bite in the air, the sun was out. A perfect day for a drive into the Gatineau Mountains. He lowered the top of his Porsche, and we zoomed along a winding road. The pure freshness of the wind, and the warm feeling of sun flowing through my body just melted me.

Finally, after three hours of driving, we turned off the main road and up a long driveway. At the end of it, tucked well back from the road, was a quaint, gray stone summer cottage. Ivy vines grew up the wall, maple trees and brush grew on two sides, and there was a nice, blue lake at the rear. St. Jacques opened the front door.

What I saw inside changed the relaxed mood the country atmosphere had set. A long wooden table was set up with drug paraphernalia—strainers, quinine, milk sugar, and caps, all in different bins. Instantly, I knew what the cottage really was: a packaging lab, where heroin was cut for street sales. Because I had a trained eye, I knew what was there, but if a legitimate person with no knowledge in the drug area were to walk into the cottage, all they would see would be a lot of junk on the table.

St. Jacques was cutting the "smack" American style—one part heroin to five part filler. So, for instance, one cut would consist of three tablespoons of quinine, two of milk sugar and one of heroin. You can visually see the difference between the substances. Quinine is shiny and flaky. Milk sugar looks like a fine, white powder. At the start, the heroin should be 80% pure so you'll always come out with a quality product. Generally, once the heroin is mixed, if it has a grayish tinge to it, you're certain of getting pretty heady stuff.

The color of heroin differs, depending upon where it comes from. Asian heroin is usually dirty white, with a gray tint. Sometimes it's pure white, like #4 China White, the purest, most sought-after heroin in the world. Then there's Indian and Mexican smack, which are both brown. St. Jacques told me that he was getting his stuff from Southeast Asia.

St. Jacques was packaging his smack the way a lot of Canadian street suppliers do—in the caps, pill casings you can buy in any drug store.

Deadly serious, St. Jacques asked, "You feel comfortable running a factory?"

"Fine with me." I wasn't lying.

It was a system that I knew well, the same one I'd used when I ran the factory for Richard Hill. The only difference was that in America, the smack was packaged in glycerin bags, like the type used to carry stamps.

When I got back into the city, I called Constable Talman. It was time to report in.

Not long afterward, I saw Talman. "You did a great job," he said "You know, I'd really like to see St. Jacques's lab," he went on.

"Look, he used a lot of backroads to get there. I'm not sure I can retrace the route," I objected.

"Try. I need to see the place in advance to figure out where to position the boys when the time comes for the bust."

Late that afternoon, with me along, Talman drove his car out of the city. The good weather we'd been having had passed and it turned into a dark, cold night.

We drove around the Gatineaus for awhile, looking for the right road, the one that would lead to the cottage. As I'd suspected, it was nothing more than a fruitless exercise, especially in the dark.

After we'd gotten lost for the umpteenth time, Talman pulled the car over and parked under an oak tree. We sat in the car talking a while then, he got out, then went to the trunk, took out a six pack and strode back.

Inside the car again, he sat closer to me.

"You know, there's lots of things I can do for you to make your life easier, Dorothy, and then again, there's lots of things I can do to make it difficult," he said, drinking his beer while taking my hand and putting it firmly in his crotch. I pulled it away.

"It might be in your best interests to comply," he said menacingly.

I knew what that meant. If I didn't do what he wanted, he would blow my cover. I could say no, but I had no doubt Talman would do just what he said. And if he did that, the RCMP wouldn't back me up. They played by their own rules.

Angry and bitter, I agreed.

Next thing I knew, I was in the backseat, with him on top of me, his stinking breath in my face. And then he was entering me and I was someplace else, someplace far and distant and long way away from here, waiting to be saved by the hero mounted on the handsome horse, absorbed in the beat of the horse's hooves as my rescuer got closer and closer.

After blackmailing me into having sex with him, he and his partner Harry Minors approached me with another pandering request.

"We don't like Inspector Stephan Deneuve," Minors began, referring to their superior who was in charge of the entire operation.

"Yeah, what we want is for you to set him up," Albert Talman continued.

"See, Stephan is a ladies man."

"And what we want you to do is entice him, under professional pretenses, to meet you for cocktails. Then, you take it from there. Do whatever you have to get him to this motel—"

"We'll tell you which one—" Minors interrupted.

". . . Right, and then, when you get him to the motel, you leave the door open and say you have to make a call to a friend."

"And you'll be that friend?" I responded.

"Right, and Minors and me'll show up and catch the Inspector with his pants down. That'll give us enough to work with."

"Work with" was another way of saying blackmail. It seemed that Stephan Deneuve was inhibiting their ability to run illegal scams on the side. To be successful, they needed him out of the way. If they could report him for conduct unbecoming, he'd be transferred out of their department.

"You do this for us Dorothy and—"

"We'll be mighty grateful," Talman finished with a sincere smile.

I thought about what they said.

"So what do you say, Dorothy?" Minors asked brightly.

That was my moment of clarity.

"What do I say? What do I say? I say, fuck you guys. I'm leaving."

I quit the project and went into headquarters to see Deneuve. I spent the first couple of minutes filling him on their offer and shady activities.

"Not only did they want to set you up, those guys are so crooked, they're ripping off street punks and taking drugs from the buys and selling it on their own," I told him. "And I'm prepared to go public."

Deneuve nodded and took it right up the line to his superiors. They initiated an internal investigation.

When I next saw Stephan Deneuve, he was packing his things in a cardboard box and clearing out his office.

"The investigation's still going on, but I've been transferred to an administrative role with the 'musical ride,'" he said simply.

The "musical ride" is insider lingo for the traveling circus of formally dressed, red-serged Mounties on horseback that travels the world promoting the RCMP.

He wasn't the only one having trouble. I had problems of my own. For reporting Minors and Talman, the RCMP treated me like a pariah. Walking through headquarters, it was apparent I was getting the silent treatment. No one talked to me.

"That's her," I could hear some of the troops muttering.

"Yeah, she's really one to be trusted," said another, loud enough so I could hear him.

Later, a friend in the organization reminded me that the major mandate of the RMCP was their code of secrecy. And whoever broke it, whatever the reason, had to be punished.

CHAPTER FOURTEEN

The Sikh Terrorist Cells

With the internal investigation of the division going on, I had some down time, and I was finally able to look a little bit closer into the activities of Michael Singh Awalia, the cab driver who drove me that first night to Le Bistro.

Since the first day we had met, Michael had become my regular taxi driver.

Because of his pager, I had easy access to him day and night. I would go to a phone and page him. Soon, his cab would tool around the corner. I waved.

"Dorothy, good to see you," Michael said brightly. "Where to this time?"

Michael drove me all over Ottawa. The places he drove me to he knew by reputation as players hang-outs. Sometimes, I invited him in for a drink. He would accept, and be impressed because some of the places were private social clubs, owned and operated by the Mafia. On his own, he never could have gotten in.

I always had money and gave him big tips. After a while, he became very curious about my activities. As we were getting to know each other, he started to cautiously share his political and religious views with me. I'm not really interested in politics, so

203

for a time, it all washed right over me, until I began to read things in the papers that tied in with something Michael had told me.

Michael began to take me to lunch at an Indian restaurant where he and his taxi driving pals would gather and sit for hours over lunch, talking about their homeland.

The place had just six or seven tables, plainly decorated. The food was traditional Indian fare, but it seemed they were there more to talk than to eat.

"We need to have our rights as Sikhs recognized," Michael would say.

"Yes, and we need to have a voice in government," another chimed in.

"We want our homeland, a Sikh homeland," a third member of the lunch party declared.

"No matter what it takes," said Michael.

"No matter, no matter," the others nodded their heads in agreement.

They were talking about very incriminating matters in front of me. When I mentioned this to Michael, he replied, "My friends know I would never bring someone among them that was not respected."

I took that to mean the same as when the Mafia said it. I was trusted. I was in.

Michael was also trying to find a place for me in his group because by now, he believed I was in the drug game. He also knew that I was well-connected just by the time he spent with me and the people I knew. But while Michael evaluated me, I was evaluating him.

I knew that taxi drivers had to work at least twelve hours a day to make a living. Yet Michael and his friends hardly drove. They met every day during their shifts and spent hours together in parking lots, restaurants and bars. All they did was visit.

Obviously, taxi driving was a front. Taxi driving gave them a reason to be on the streets; they were always mobile. No one would notice a taxi in any part of the city, any time of the day.

And the daily meetings continued. It seemed that someone would talk to India every day and report to the group. Some days, they were very happy with the news. Others, they crucified the Indian government, specifically Indira Gandhi.

"She has to die," one Sikh zealot would assert, and the others would pound the table in agreement.

Sometimes, things got very crazy. They would act out how Indira would/should die. As for me, I was involved because I was a player. They wanted my help—drugs, explosives, guns, money laundering. All of this was to generate money to support their revolution back home and to train their people abroad. They picked my brain, and I gave them just enough info to show that I was cooperating, but nothing they could not find out if they visited the library and knew where to look.

By now, I believed that they were terrorists. The way they talked about weapons convinced me. Everyone of them had served in the Indian army. Only weapons experts could have the in-depth conversations they had about killing machines.

I had successfully infiltrated a Sikh terrorist cell in the midst of Canada. It was information that should have been passed onto the RCMP, but since I was having my problems with that esteemed organization, I had no one to pass the information on to. A few days later in the restaurant, even more important information came my way.

"It's on," Michael said simply.

"The Prime Minister?"

"Yes. Details are in the final stages."

Living the life I lived, I heard daily that someone was going to kill somebody or hurt someone. Violent language and threats were common most of the time. They were just idle boasting. But every once in awhile, I heard something which my gut told me was true. I was never wrong. There would be an air of certainty. That day in the Indian restaurant, I knew this was one of those times.

Once a very hot July day, I sat in a stifling bar, dressed in a cool, crisp, cotton short sleeved blouse over light, cotton mid-thigh shorts. I was very tan, and the cream and white of my outfit set it off nicely. I pulled my long hair back from my face. It was too hot for all that hair —I should get it cut, I thought, waiting for Michael.

When Michael picked me up, he was wearing lightweight black slacks and a mustard colored golf shirt. I sighed. Michael was well-built. He lifted weights, and it showed. He was also very handsome. Back home in Calcutta, he had acted in a few movies.

"I would have continued my movie career if the Khalistani movement didn't need me," he said as he tooled the car around a curve.

The heart of the Sikh movement was a push to separate from India and establish an independent, theocratic nation called Khalistan, which means "Land of the Pure." The Prime Minister was against such a move. Indeed, the hand of fate started to rest on her head after she ordered the attack on the Sikh's holiest shrine, the Golden Temple in Amritsar, in June of 1984. She had ordered the attack in order to flush out Sikh terrorists, who had taken sanctuary inside the temple. It had been a terribly bloody confrontation.

I noticed as we approached the restaurant that Michael was more serious than usual.

"Can I trust you?"

Why was he asking me that now? I looked him straight in the eye.

"What do you think?"

He seemed tortured in his spirit. We parked the car without another word between us. All the other guys were there already. They, too, were unusually serious.

A message had been sent to the Prime Minister. It was custom any to warn the victim ahead of time. A note had been placed on his pillow in his bed chambers. The note said:

If we can get this close to you, we can kill you anytime.

In the restaurant, one of the men asked Michael, "What's a good time?"

"It has to be before Christmas," Michael answered, and they all agreed on a day in October. The method of execution had already been agreed upon by the Sikh terrorist leaders throughout the world.

"Gunfire," Michael told me.

"The only sure way to execute someone, and to be sure they don't survive, is a suicide attack," said another.

"Someone close to her," Michael nodded.

So they already had the details planned out.

That was enough. I couldn't let the Prime Minister die when I knew what was in store for her. Immediately, I contacted the RCMP and passed on the information.

The RCMP is never happy when an outsider is closer to the action than they are. So they always slice and dice any information an agent gathers. In so doing, they have been known to shoot themselves in the foot. I was sure, however, that they would pass on the information to the proper authorities and someone would act to save her.

Six months later, on a frosty fall morning, I arose about 11:00. I didn't want to think about anything more important than brewing a cup of coffee. I bent down and picked up the newspaper under the front door. A newspaper headline blared out the word "assassinated."

I hate reading the paper before breakfast. Who wants to start their day with blood and guts? Years earlier, I'd made it a rule not to read the paper until later in the day, when I was better able to cope with the problems of the world. But something about that word, on this day, some instinct— call it what you want, made me break my own rule and look.

As I read, my mouth felt like dry cotton. I couldn't catch a breath. Even though my ice pick was safely tucked away in my dresser, I felt like someone was running it up and down my spine, the cold metal making my skin tingle. I raced to the bathroom and made it in time to throw up bile from my empty, knotted stomach and all over the toilet.

The newspaper story read:

"The 66-year-old prime minister was shot at by two members of his own security detail. She had come out of his house in the morning to make a video recording when suddenly, out of the blue, two persons carrying Sten guns, shot her eight to ten times. The Prime Minister fell down with a cry. The two assassins were instantly shot dead by other security guards.

"She was immediately rushed to the hospital. One of the guards allegedly involved in the shooting was identified as Satwant Singh. Singh, which means "lion" in Punjabi, is part of the name of virtually every Sikh."

The information I had given the RCMP was very time and detail specific. Whether the RCMP passed on my information, I will never know, but three facts are indisputable: one, the RCMP knew that a hit was going to take place before it did; two, the RCMP knew that it was going to be perpetrated by someone close to the Prime Minister; and three, Mrs. Gandhi had indeed been assassinated. Why then, knowing all this, had she not been saved?

I would never know.

Whatever the reason, Mrs. Gandhi had died. I had tried to prevent her assassination and failed.

It was the first time, on this side of the law, that I felt responsible for another person's death.

CHAPTER FIFTEEN

The Jamaican Posse

The next few years sped by. I worked job after job; always in disguise, always in the line of fire. My reputation grew. A lot of bad people were looking for me, but they never knew who I was or where. When I arrived in Calgary, it was a very good time for the economy there due to the oil boom.

Party palaces were opening all over town. European chefs were wooed to town with the promise of the very good life to be matched with very good salaries. And they came, along with designers, architects, doctors and lawyers, all the professions, to reap the spoils of prosperity.

Because of the oil boom, the city was flooded with money from oilmen, speculators and grifters, and the loose morals that comes with sudden wealth. The hookers came and some set up trailers close to the "Patch," the city's Times Square, so they could catch the "Rig Pigs," the truck drivers, on the way to Calgary on payday. High class call girls rented posh apartments and hotel suites in the better establishments. They catered to the oil pushers and ranchers. Some of the oil companies even had call girls on the payroll.

Then there were the gangsters. They could smell money a continent away. They came to add to their coffers. The Mob stays liquid because of their ability to pounce on opportunity. An oil boom was reason enough to salivate.

Prostitution, protection, extortion, gambling. But the biggest money maker of all was—cocaine. Half the players had it and the other half wanted it. For the police, a plan to buy and bust was not feasible. They could not handle the turnover. As soon as the ink was dry, the perp would be back on the street selling his poison. Because the dealers were floaters, they wouldn't show for court and the cops did not have the manpower to go after bail jumpers. And even if they did, they wouldn't have gotten their man. The perp had already taken a powder.

The city couldn't keep their officers tied up for hours at a time doing paperwork on buys and busts. The RCMP was in the same boat, too, so they went operational.

"Dorothy, we need you," said Brad Parker, a lieutenant in Calgary RCMP's narcotics division.

"What do you need?"

"We want to bust the Jamaican posses."

Posses are gangs of Jamaicans who run together.

"They're responsible for most of the drugs coming into Calgary," Brad continued. "Those are your targets, them and their boys."

Back when I was active in the drug trade, I used to fly back and forth with twenty pounds of marijuana at a time from Jamaica.

I carried it in my luggage and positioned myself at a predesignated spot in the luggage claim area, where an airport employee snatched it surreptitiously and bring it around, bypassing customs. Then, after safely clearing customs, I met him and my people in the parking lot. I'll say one thing for the Jamaicans: they were very well organized.

It was through such dealings that I gained the confidence of the Jamaican posses. They accepted me as one of their own, and at my insistence, my partner Harold as well.

While posses are popularly known as marijuana smugglers, they also deal heavily in other drugs, especially cocaine. The Calgary project was mostly cocaine.

It sounded good. I was to infiltrate the posse, set up some major drug buys with as many of the main players as I could involve, then the boys would move in for the arrests. With a little bit of luck, we could put them out of commission for awhile.

I became an agent again. Brad gave me the standard agreement that all crown agents signed. It stipulated how much I would be paid and what my expenses would be. I signed the document, kept a copy for myself and gave him back the original.

For this job, I got as much sun as I could to make my skin look darker. I teased my hair into dreadlocks and wore the type of drop waisted dresses Jamaican women favor.

Disguise in place, it was time to establish myself as a player. Andre's was a downtown bar that intelligence told us was frequented by members of the Jamaican posses.

"Hey mon, how ya do?"

"Nice sister, real nice," said a Jamaican who was sizing me up at the bar.

"How you called?"

"Dorothy. You mon?"

"Robin."

"Well Robin, nice to meet you."

We continued drinking in silence, Robin giving me the once over. I turned back to him and smiled coquettishly.

"What your family name, mon?"

"Why?" He looked at me suspiciously.

"You look familiar."

"Where your family from?"

"Kingston."

"You for Readie or Lakes?"

Jamaicans take their democracy very seriously. They are zealots about their political preferences. It's not uncommon during election time for deaths to result from the conflict. Thomas

Readie had been prime minister until Kurt Lakes defeated him. Each had their own militant constituency in the Kingston slums. I had no idea which side Robin favored.

"Lakes," I said firmly, going with the winner.

Robin smiled and clapped me on the back. "You a good woman."

"Well, got to go now. Back to work."

"Hey, what kind work you do?"

I just smiled and walked out.

Over the next couple of days, I went into a few more of the bars where the posses hung out. I talked to the men in the same way I had with Robin, letting drop I was looking for some work. By the time I got back to Andre's bar, Robin had already heard from his friends that I was in the market for work in some discrete criminal enterprise.

"I hear you lookin' for some money work?"

"Who you hear from, Robin?"

"Never mind, Dorothy. How I know you qualified?"

"What am I applying for?"

"Prime Minister."

We both laughed.

"I could do a better job that any of them."

"I don't doubt that. But hey, you ever do any, aah—"

"Drug work?"

"I didn't say that."

"No, you didn't. And yes, I did: in New York. I ran a factory for Richard Hill."

"He big mon."

"Used to be. He's dead now. I also did some work with Cadillac Richie Wheeler."

Robin sucked in his breath. He was impressed, and why not? I was telling the truth. Telling a lie always works better when you use part of the truth.

"So you looking for work? Well, we need couriers."

"Who's 'we'?"

"I work for Arthur Townsend."

Bingo. One of my targets. I tried to contain my excitement, but as we made up to meet again and get down to some heavier business discussions, I knew that, with my cover established, it was time to bring in my partner, the undercover police agent, Harold Morrison.

"You look like a guy I used to know," I told Harold, who in tone, manner and deportment was the spitting image of Josh La Forge. I wasn't surprised. There must be some giant machine working overtime spitting out naive police agents, I thought.

I almost never went to work without a weapon, sometimes even a gun. The RCMP didn't want me armed, since I was a civilian agent, but I made my own decisions. I only packed a gun when I believed that my life was in danger, but I almost always carried my friend, the ice pick.

Now understand, every time I went out on assignment my life was in jeopardy, but sometimes I knew in advance that a deal could go sour because of the personalities and egos of the players involved. Then I made sure to carry. That night I was baby-sitting another amateur undercover cop. And nothing can get you hurt faster than an amateur.

Despite my street smart talk and manner, I violated my own rule and gone out that night without a weapon because I figured I might be searched. I tried to relax and pushed my anxious thoughts about being unarmed into my subconscious.

At midnight, dressed in a tight orange dress with gold hoop earrings and donning a new black wig, I went to The Island Bar, a hip dance club that had a multicolored dance floor with flashing lights and a revolving disco globe suspended from the ceiling. Harold accompanied me. As we went inside to check on our traps, I glanced down the street.

We had a cover team of six men in three unmarked cars and they were parked outside waiting for us to make a deal or, like most nights, prime the pump for the days to come. The officers inside the car were probably reading the paper. Only on our signal would they move in.

The music coming from a 1950's jukebox was loud and unintelligible. The lights were dim, probably so no one would notice how much the drinks were being watered down. The players in the place were mostly blacks and Italians. A lot of them were cokeheads.

Most of the young women scattered around were middle class working girls out for some easy action. They had seen too many reruns of detective shows on TV and were convinced they wanted to be in the fast lane. If they only knew that the price they would eventually pay for that privilege was a pact with 'Old Scratch: He would supply the sex and the drugs and the booze and they would allow their souls to be leached out of their bodies bit by bit till nothing was left. But I was not a social worker. My job was to get as much poison off the streets as I could and put the pushers behind bars. If some giggly, jiggly, wiggly young wannabe got saved because of my efforts, that was just an added bonus.

The RCMP also didn't want to lose contact with any of the bad guys we had hit in the weeks before. We always needed to know where everyone was and if they were still active. Damage control was one of our primary responsibilities. After all, we, the forces representing law and order, were allowing Mr. Pusher to keep selling drugs for almost two years in some cases, in the hopes he'd lead us to Mr. Big.

While we waited to enact a plan we had for a major buy, I started to ponder the pros and cons. There is a school of thought within the law enforcement community that holds that buy and bust is the best way to go, because it takes the bad guy off the street immediately. I understand that thinking. But it also exposes the undercover and/or crown agent working on the project for only one buy because we have to testify in court. Also, the pusher is out on bond immediately, so what the hell is stopped, really? If, instead, we can prove a pattern and also use the pusher to take us to his or her man by putting in an order too big for him to handle, it takes the case to a higher level. More good, I think, is done that way in the long run.

Still, there are bound to be some first-time users while we're putting the big bust together. Some would say that we allowed it to happen by not arresting Mr. Pusher in the first place, but let's be frank. We can only do so much, and it's people who do nothing that always offer their informed opinion first.

I looked over at my U. C. Harold, however, was not into introspection. He had hit the bar almost immediately, slugging down Southern Comfort Manhattans. Some of the posse members were across the room and I knew they were watching us. The last thing I needed was for Harold to get blotto and start shooting his mouth off, but soon, he was drunk out of his mind.

"Hey this is a stinkin' place," he yelled out.

He'd been getting louder and louder as the alcohol took hold. A lot of people get confrontational when drinking, and Harold was worse than most.

"Hey mon, why you not shut up?" Robin yelled from across the room.

Harold looked at him, smiled and slugged down another drink. Robin's eyes met mine. I shrugged my shoulders.

The faces of the posses members, whose egos I'd been massaging on previous visits, turned toward Harold with enough hostility to kill. I strode over to them.

"Hey mon, he's just a stupid white boy," I said.

"Hey mon, that guy is asking for it," said Franklin, one of Robin's men.

I could only watch as Harold got into a fistfight with Tony Caprio, a member of the Italian Mob. Great. Just great.

"Watch what the Italian does to him," said Robin. He smiled. He and Caprio may have come from different worlds, but he had a real professional respect for the mobster.

Wonderful, I thought. One creep admires another. My job now was to keep the Jamaicans cool, so they wouldn't mix in and so Harold would have a fighting chance.

Watching him scarf down drink and after drink got me God damn mad. Sure, sometimes you have to fight, but that bastard could have gotten me killed by drinking too much and losing control. It was just so unprofessional, but you know what? If I'd died trying to help him, the RCMP probably would never even have claimed me as one of theirs. Another cover up would have happened.

When I next looked over, Harold was getting the shit kicked out him. Then my subconscious released my former anxiety. I wasn't armed. That knowledge chilled me to the bone.

But I had no choice. Harold was my partner. Despite his stupidity, I had to help him anyway.

"Hey guys, I got some business to attend to over there, so how 'bout staying out of this one?" I said to the Jamaicans. They agreed, but only because they knew their leader, Arthur Townsend, had the hots for me.

Caprio's boots were connecting with Harold's stomach when I threw the beer bottle. It shattered against the side of his head. Glass and blood began raining down on his face. I'd opened his face real bad, like all those years ago with the razor blades and the kids in the school yard. Caprio, too, stopped in his tracks.

Harold got his second wind. He was on his feet, Caprio's mob buddies, seeing their friend in trouble, were closing in fast. No time to run, I thought.

I rushed to Harold's side. There we were, fighting side by side for our very lives. We began fighting our way to the door, feet, fists, bottles and glasses were our weapons. I felt something slice through my thumb but there was no pain. Whatever it was, it'd been razor sharp. Then I felt something warm oozing down my wrist, and looked down. Blood was gushing out.

Outside, the cover team sat in their cars stuffing their faces with coffee and donuts. They couldn't know anyway because we didn't have any toys (wires) on us. The only communications device was in the car itself. Also, a cover team cannot and will not move unless the undercover people give them the signal for help. At that time, the project is burned, we have to fold our tents and go back to the desert. No one wants that, and I surely didn't, so we fought on.

Now, if I didn't get involved and make a hard hit right off, the club lights would have dimmed, which is the custom to give the favorite a chance to stick the trouble maker real good, and when the lights would come back on, everyone would be standing away from the body like nothing had happened. This would have definitely happened in the Island Bar because the owner was a woman friend of Caprio's. Besides, Harold was the new kid on the block and no one was on his side . . . except me.

I looked over. Harold was bleeding profusely from a cut over his right eye. We made it outside and I coaxed him into the car we were using and managed to get to the hospital.

"That thumb needs stitches," said the emergency room doctor. He was looking at my right thumb. One of our friends back at the bar had sliced through to the bone.

The doctor began probing and pressing my ribs. I grunted in pain.

"Well, you're pretty banged up," he said. "But you're lucky. No broken ribs. You'll probably be urinating blood for awhile. You took some awfully hard shots to the kidney."

I looked down at my torso. A good part of it had already turned black and blue.

Harold, though, fared even worse. His eye was seriously damaged and so was his knee. And if I hadn't stopped Caprio, he would have beaten Harold to death. Still, I wasn't about to let our battered physical conditions impede our goals. I was ready to go right back into the war zone.

Robert had introduced me to his boss, and my target, Arthur Townsend. So far he hadn't done anything we could use against him. He was too busy trying to get into my pants, but I knew that sooner or later, he'd give me some drugs to take down to New York. Bottom line, he could have any girl he wanted; I was around because of my criminal contacts.

Sure enough, one day a few weeks after the fight in the Island Bar, Arthur called me over to his apartment. It was tastefully furnished in beiges and blues, simple but elegant, with a lot of rosewood.

"Dorothy, I'd like you to do a little job for me."

I leaned forward. We were sitting on a sofa. His men, including Robin, were stationed around the room.

"Robin, bring it in."

Robin went into the next room quickly and when he came back, he had a package tied up in plain wrapping paper.

"I want you to take this to New York. Our friends in the Bonanno Family are expecting it."

"Blow?" I asked.

Arthur nodded.

He handed it over. It had to weigh at least twenty kilos. Depending on purity, its street value could be in the millions. We'd already bought a lot of that shit from Arthur's men, but this was the first time Arthur himself had stuck his neck out.

"Don't worry Arthur, I'll take care of everything."

I kissed him gently on the cheek. Just then, the door burst open. Harold and the cover team entered with guns drawn.

"Everyone freeze," Harold shouted.

The Jamaicans had been reaching inside their jackets for their guns but when they saw they were outnumbered, they put their hands down at their sides and allowed themselves to be cuffed.

Arthur turned back and looked at me.

"You bitch, you—"

His hand came back to slug me but he never made it. My punch hit him square on the jaw. He tumbled over to the floor. One of the Mounties rushed over and cuffed him immediately. Now it was time to cast our net out and bring in the rest of the fish.

Throughout Calvary, doors burst open in the secret lairs of the Jamaican posses.

"Freeze," the cops shouted.

A lot of the posses and the drugs they sold were taken off the streets, at least for a time. We took down a lot of bad guys. On their way up, they had already inflicted a lot of damage on innocent people. Now, they'd see what it was like to suffer.

CHAPTER SIXTEEN

Project Scorpion

My problems with some of the hierarchy at the RCMP didn't just vanish into the night. It was an ongoing battle, my word against their image, and I knew they had the will and the power to prevail.

My friend Lewis Cameron, a Mountie who had good connections, suggested I go to work for the Ottawa City Police. This would serve three purposes.

First, I would be under their protection; second, I would continue the work I'd invested so much in; and third, but not least, I would earn a living again. With my RCMP work cut off, so was my livelihood. I'd been forced to do menial labor as a dispatcher for Hail Right, the sleaziest cab company in all of Canada. Most of the drivers were small-time hoods, tapped into petty crimes. The working conditions were awful—dirty offices and dirtier bathrooms.

My biggest worry was getting caught in a raid because drugs, swag and prostitutes were sold out of the office and orders were taken over the dispatch. The taxi operation served as a criminal front. But my life was legit and as long as I didn't get involved, I was okay. I just didn't want the hassle.

I considered Lewis's suggestion, but there was a big problem: I really didn't want to work for a local police force because they didn't have the funds to work a major sting. By this time, I was

221

convinced that the only way to stop the raging drug wars was to get the top. City police could not handle the expenses incurred during such an operation.

However, one day, I was reading the newspaper and an article caught my eye. It read:

> Police have launched a major investigation into the Kaya crime family. Anyone having information regarding this matter, please notify Inspector Donald Draven of the City Police.

I knew the Kayas. In a matter of seconds, I was on the phone. "I have information on the Kayas," I told Lt. Draven.

The Kaya Family. Bert Kaya, Flint Kaya and Farradin Kaya. There are more, but these three brothers were the main targets. They were also in tight with some big names. For example, Sarah Trudeau, the wife of the prime minister, was one of the Kayas' friends. Neither the Kayas nor Sarah could do anything to enhance the others image, but the drug culture caused them to become friends.

Unfortunately, the Kayas soon discovered that hanging around with Sarah was not to their advantage. Wherever she went, the press with their prying cameras and questions followed. The Kayas wanted to be known and feared within the underworld, but being in the public eye was not good for business. They cut Sarah loose and off she went to find some other, less camera-shy friends.

After I told Inspector Draven who I was and some of what I knew, he said we should meet for lunch.

"Don't worry, they don't know my face," he assured me. "I'm basically a desk cop."

The last thing I needed was to be seen having lunch with a cop. Grudgingly, I accepted his invitation.

"Look, the bad guys still don't have a clue as to who I am. I want to keep it that way. "

"I'd be the last to want to blow your cover," he insisted.

"Let's meet at Peking Palace, a Chinese restaurant I know." I gave him the address.

At our meeting, I found the Inspector to be very personable.

"It is a pleasure to finally meet you. The news of your work has given you a respected if somewhat, aah—"

"Mysterious?" I smiled.

"Right," he smiled back, "a mysterious reputation in our circles."

"I'm not surprised," I said, and told him a little about my problems with the RCMP.

"I've heard horror stories about some of them before," he reassured me. I sighed heavily. It was good to find someone in the police community who believed me. I told him some of the information I had on the Kayas.

"Very interesting," he commented. "You certainly seem to have a good understanding of their psyches. Give me your phone number in case we have some more questions."

I did, and figured that was the end of it. I'd done my civic duty and had a lovely lunch. So I was surprised when, later in the week, I received a call from him.

"Hello, Dorothy? It's Inspector Draven."

"How are you, Inspector?"

"Fine, thank you. Dorothy, I'd like you to make a date to meet with one of my men. His name is Byron Smith. Constable Smith is a drug investigator and he's very interested in what you know about the Kayas."

"Sure, I'd be glad to, but the first thing we have to do is find a safe place for the meet. Byron's a street cop, right?"

"Right."

"Then all the dealers know him. All right, let's set up the meeting at night. That's the only time I'll feel comfortable."

"You know best."

Two days later, as darkness settled on the city, Byron Smith picked me up in front of my apartment building. He drove to a nearby suburb and found a bar to stop at. We went in, had a few Guinesses and chit-chatted for almost an hour. I was acting antsy when he finally turned to the real reason for our meeting.

"We have a big project in mind," he said.

"The city won't pay for it," I said firmly.

"Yeah, you're right. We're taking it higher up."

"Tell me about it," I countered. He outlined the plan.

"We've dubbed the operation Scorpion. We have a target list of known Mafia players and we'll add to it as we go along. The paper trail we have came from the Intelligence Division, which gathered it from a number of sources: investigators, call-ins, paid informants and agents in the field."

"Sometimes the intelligence matches what's found in the field, sometime not," I reminded him.

He nodded.

"No one has to be lying," I went on. "It's just that everyone does not know everything at the same time. The agent is the only one who is undercover months before the police undercover comes along. By the time the u.c. enters the picture, I've already been in the homes of most of the targets."

Byron laughed.

"Look, your project sounds good and I've got a lot to bring to it. All the targets I met when working for the Feds I can give to you."

Byron smiled again. I trusted him immediately. He was a professional.

"Let me make this clear, Byron. I need some rope if you want me to produce all I can."

Byron held up his hand. "I understand. There won't be any problems, Dorothy." He signaled for the check.

"By the way. Who's the project's big target?"

"One of the Mafia's finest. Nicky Pugliese," Byron said, opening his wallet.

Nicky. We hadn't seen each other since he'd tried to recruit me years before. Meanwhile, his star had risen.

In bed that night, I thought over the newest project to which I'd committed myself. As far as the operation was concerned, contacting Nicky would be the least of my worries. He knew me, so my criminal background with him was already established. The hardest part would be bringing an undercover into one of the very biggest crime families during a very difficult time.

In countries around the world, the Mafia families were splintering. The young bloods were opposing the old guard, the old way of doing things. Some of them were acting as free agents. Not only did this disturb the status quo, more importantly it meant the family bank was not being fed.

Canada's lax immigration laws made it a perfect place to settle. Different Mafia families, including the Ianniluccis, Zappias, and the Camisios, had scattered all across southern Ontario. They weren't loyal to the same don. All of them were trying to build their own crime families, trying to grow faster than the rest, and become a power base so strong and connected that the lesser families would fall in line behind them. It was a struggle for power, and it was a very dangerous time to be around the Mafia.

The action on the streets of Ottawa was as fierce as anything in the Chicago of the 1930's. Mob members flew back and forth to Italy and Sicily. More came in from Hamilton, Ontario, Toronto, Montreal and the United States.

Blood was hot and roots ran deep. The old men cursed the drugs, but they had long gotten over their ethical problems about dealing in the poison; they had come to see that a fortune could be made. This, of course, was their overriding "raison d etre" and without a seconds hesitation, they took control of the trade. As for the young turks revolting against them, they had to be brought to heel.

What was known and acknowledged as fact was that Nicky was one of those young turks, a big time drug dealer, who had split from the Calabrian mob he had been born into. The local police and the feds on both sides of the border had been trying to bust Nicholas Pugliese for ten years. No one could get close enough to him to get the goods. The words slick, smooth, sharp and smart were always thrown around when the cops talked about Nicky. He was still out there and a major target of the operation. They hadn't busted him before Scorpion because they couldn't make anything stick. Now it was my turn to right this wrong.

There is so much security surrounding a project, it can make you crazy. The first thing you need is a safe house. The reason the base of operations had to be moved from the main police building was that other police officers cannot know what's going on, in case there's a leak.

In police terms, a safe house is a totally secure place, an office away from the main office, where a team of officers can do their paperwork, eat, sleep, make phone calls and the undercover people can receive calls from their contacts. It's a safe place where all the team members can meet out of sight. The team is handpicked and everyone prays that there are no leaks. But there always are. Why?

A safe house promotes pillow talk. Here's the formula:

SEX + BEER + COPS = LEAKS

Unfortunately, cops tend to tell their lovers all kinds of stuff they shouldn't, and then their lovers tell God-knows-who and that's how security can get compromised.

High rise apartments are the best place for a safe house because they're not noticeable from the street when people come and go, or where exactly in the building they are going. Often, the members get off on different floors and walk up or down several floors to the safe house. That way, there's no pattern, though after awhile, the teams gets careless or tired and everyone comes on at the same time, rides in the same elevator or gets off on the same floor. Any tenant who's observant may inadvertently say something that could lead to the discovery of a police team living in the building, which means the safe house is burned.

It's not easy finding a safe house. Scorpion was no exception. Finally, we found an apartment house on the edge of the city that looked ideal for our purposes. All the tenants were checked out to make sure none had criminal backgrounds. The last thing we needed was a cop working on the job to be fingered by one of the tenants. That would blow everything.

Then the owner was checked out. As with the tenants, clean. On Scorpion, we needed not one, but two apartments.

On the top floor of the six story building, we established the actual safe house where the cops would work. However, what we did a little differently was to bring the technical boys in to wire video and audio equipment from the safe house to an apartment one floor directly below us.

In the middle of the night, so as not to alert the neighbors, the techies came in with their eavesdropping equipment. Hidden cameras were carefully concealed behind mirrors and bookcases that were specially designed for these purposes. A few days later, a furniture delivery company arrived with beds, sofas, kitchen sets, everything needed to furnish the apartment. Finally, the new tenant, Jay Norloff, a brown-haired, blue-eyed boy from Manitoba, moved in.

It was time for me to go to work.

Nicky still hung out at the same social club. It wasn't hard to find him.

"Hey, the lady with brass balls," Nicky said, his hand raised in greeting when he saw me.

"Nicky. I hear you're moving up."

"Course I am, course I am," he said proudly. All those Mafia guys loved to have their egos stroked. "And looking to move even higher."

"So I've heard. Everyone's talking about you."

He smiled. "And I heard about you. I hear you're dealing coke now."

Between my regular criminal contacts and those of the police, it was easy to get the word out on the street that I was a mid-level coke dealer. Since I actually socialized and lived among the criminal community, no one ever questioned my pedigree.

"Well, considering you're big time and I'm small time —'"

Nicky laughed.

"—I thought maybe you and I could strike a deal."

"You're not competition for me?"

"No one could compete against you, Nicky."

"True."

"Why don't you come over to this place I'm using."

"Is it safe?"

"Don't insult my intelligence."

"You know, Dorothy, you're the only woman I'd deal with."

"Because you respect me so much?"

"No, because you got such a smart mouth. If I had to 'hit' you, I wouldn't mind."

"Unlike most women, who your code of honor prevents you from killing, even if they screw you."

"Exactly." What a hypocrite.

The next day, Nicky came over to the apartment.

"Nice place," he said, looking around, admiring the tapestries on the walls.

"Thanks. It's a friend's. Listen, while we talk, I need three ounces of your best blow."

"A grand an ounce."

"No problem."

Nicky left and was back fifteen minutes later with the drugs. We exchanged. He didn't bother to count the money while I tasted the stuff. This was the appetizer: assessing each other before we settled down to the main meal.

"Good, right?"

"Mmm."

228

We talked for an hour more about how things had changed in the business.

"You know, it's like New York was in the '20's when Luciano took over and killed the old mustache Petes. That's what oughta happen now."

"Maybe somebody with the balls oughta do it," I said.

Nicky grinned.

The next time we were at the apartment, I told him about Jay.

"He's my partner. He's in California now. This is actually his place. We been doing deals together for ten years in Florida, all over the States, South America, you name it."

"Yeah. So what?"

"So he can lay a lot of stuff off on his connections in the States."

"I don't think so. I don't like new people."

What he really meant was a new person could be a cop. Or an assassin. My job was to convince him to meet Jay.

"Are you in business or what? This guy can make you money."

"I got money."

"Well, how about a lot more?"

The third time Nicky came to the apartment for a deal, we were just exchanging money for drugs when the phone rang.

"Hello?"

"Time."

"Jay. Great. You're back early. How did it go?"

"Wonderful. You think he's ready?"

"Yeah. Wait, I'll see."

I cupped the receiver.

"Nicky, it's Jay. He got in early from Los Angeles. He said it'd take him about thirty minutes to get in from the airport. Want to meet him?"

It had to be Nicky's idea, but one I'd planted. I appealed to his sense of greed.

"Come on, this guy can make you money." I stretched out the "m" word for effect.

"Ah what the hell, ya got any booze around here?"

I smiled and turned back to the receiver..

"Yeah, Jay, Nicky's going to hang around. But make it fast. You know he's a busy man."

I went to the bar and poured him a Courvoisier. Thirty minutes later to the minute, we heard the key turning in the door and Jay walked in.

"Nicholas Pugliese, meet Jay Norloff."

With "nice to meet yous" all around, they settled on the couch, Nicky sniffing his brandy.

"So Dorothy tells me you sold us some stuff while I was gone?"

"Yeah," said Nicky noncommittally.

We didn't want to spook him, so the conversation turned mundane until Nicky said he had to go. But he was back a week later for another transaction, and this time, they got down to business.

"That's penny ante stuff, you know," Nicky said, turning over a few ounces. Jay handed him the money in return.

"I know it is. It's for some private clients."

"Dorothy says you can lay off a lot of stuff."

"Sure can. Can you supply it?"

"I can get you any amount you want. I'm the biggest," Nicky bragged.

That was my cue. I excused myself. Jay was in. Now it was up to him to set the trap.

"I got an appointment downtown. See you later, Jay."

"Bye, Dorothy," said Jay.

"You know, Dorothy, maybe it's about time we got together on something," Nicky said, grinning.

He was so damn full of himself. A stocky, blond, blue-eyed Italian in his early 30's, he considered himself to be the Robert Redford of the mob set.

"You know Nicky, you gotta stop letting your cock think for you instead of your brain," I said.

Or cocaine, I thought. Nicky was a user. He wanted me, and I let him think that though I was attracted to him, it would always be business between us. And business it was.

I left, took the stairs up a flight, took out a key and turned the lock of an apartment door. Inside, the room was crowded with ten or so men, hunkered down in front of a bank of video screens. The sound was turned up.

"Hey Dorothy, ya gotta see this," said Byron Smith, with a broad grin on his face. I walked over and watched as Constable Jay Norloff negotiated to buy a kilo of cocaine from Nicky Pugliese.

Over the next sixth months, Nicky and Jay negotiated all kinds of deals on an escalating scale, for anything from five ounces of cocaine up to multiple kilos. Once the trade got into the millions of dollars, it would be up to the police to figure out when they had made enough buys to trigger the bust. In the meanwhile, I hung out.

A good part of my job involves hanging out with the target. The more you're part of the scenery, the less they suspect you. We hung in Nicky's social club, his office, restaurants, in his fancy apartment, and in the hideouts his drug ring maintained in the Little Italy section of Ottawa.

Usually, I met him someplace, but sometimes, like that one night, he called me in my apartment. "Dorothy, this is Charlie." Charlie was Nicky's code name. He didn't like using his real name on the phone. He was afraid of being bugged. The irony wasn't lost on me.

"I'm picking you up in two minutes."

Damn! Not enough time to contact Byron or Jay and have them tail me.

Nicky picked me up and took me to one of his hideouts. The sounds of beer tabs popping and plastic chips clicking together drifted up to Nicky's lair where we lounged, above the gambling and watering hole that Nicky ran. As I looked across the room at Nicky, something struck me the wrong way. I didn't know what it was, a feeling, an instinct, that something just was not right. I looked over again at Nicky's blue eyes, glazed over from a cocaine high.

Nicky was busy caressing his new silk shirt. Pure silk. At $300 per, he had them sent over from Italy by the dozen. After selecting his favorites, he'd pass on the rest to his soldiers. "Hey Dorothy, try this out," Nicky said, as he sauntered to a table in the middle of the room. On the table were a knife and a gun. Using the knife, he began cutting coke lines.

Bending over the table, I inserted a $100 bill in my nose and pretended to snort a couple of lines. My long hair streamed down my face and neck, obstructing his view as I brushed the white powder into my lap.

"Wow, fine, real fine," I said with a beatific smile.

We weren't alone in the room. Vinnie was also there, one of Nicky's runners. Both guys were already flying so high they'd need a parachute to get down.

I shivered. I'd been alone with Nicky before. It was always an ideal situation for gathering intelligence. But something this night was giving me the creeps. Nicky was hyper ordinarily, but tonight he was more agitated than usual.

He sat down on the couch and reached over to the coffee table for the knife. The stainless steel blade glittered from reflected light. Nicky ran his thumb down the blade, his eyes crazy with delight.

"You know, you and I have never really bonded," he said, his gaze fixed on me.

"You learned a new word. Have you been seeing a shrink?" I laughed, my heart pounding.

"What are you laughing at?"

"Come on, quit kidding around," I said sternly. "We do business together. That's it, right?"

"Wrong. There's more to it than that. You know what I want."

I grimaced. Just like all the other men in my life.

"You don't need me with all the girls in your life," I replied, trying hard to appeal to his ego. "You have your pick of girls better looking than me. A lot better-looking than me. I've seen some."

"Yeah, but it's you I want." He smiled. He had strong white teeth that looked ready to bite.

"Besides," I continued, not giving up, "what if I'm not good?"

"I'll be the judge of that," he said, fondling the knife like it was his cock. "And Vinnie will, too."

Oh, shit. I'd better think fast.

"Has our friendship come to this?" I asked. "What if I just get up and walk out?"

"Well, your back would make good target practice," he said.

There was a steel edge to his voice. I believed him. If I tried to get out of there, I was dead. Nicky had killed before, when he was sober. Peaking on coke as he was now, unstable, there was no doubt in my mind that he'd kill me.

What were the odds? I had nothing, only my friend the ice pick. They both carried revolvers. I could get one maybe, but no way I could fight both of them. Not high and wired. And no one is faster than a bullet. Either I died fighting or I submitted and lived. Not much of a choice.

Without undressing, Nicky pushed me into a bed in the corner. I heard the zipper of his pants, then felt his cock brushing against my thigh. He lifted my dress, ripped my panties, and then forced himself inside me. My head turned. There was Vinnie, watching. Nicky's rhythm matched Vinnie's masturbatory motions on the knife handle.

After Nicky, it was Vinnie's turn. I closed my eyes tightly. Pain, anger, fear, flooded my body. Where was the hero I'd always dreamed would rescue me? Damn him. There was only me.

Afterwards, I lay back on the bed.

"I'll give you a ride home," said Nicky, grinning again.

I sat stoically as his sports car zoomed across the sleeping city. Finally, he parked in front of my house and leaned across the seat. His breath smelled from stale cognac.

"No hard feelings, right babe?"

Mumbling a reply, I staggered through my front door, went inside, and scrubbed from head to foot, worried that the son-of-a-bitch had given me AIDS. Nicky slept around.

I was in shock, but I wasn't going to be victimized again, not like in Chicago and so many other places in my past when I was a bad guy. I was on the right side of the law now, and my police contacts would do something to make this right. I called them.

"What the fuck were you doing with him alone?" the cops asked me.

Not, "Are you okay?" or, "Did he hurt you?"

"What the fuck were you doing with him alone?" they repeated.

Their attitude astonished me. Like I'd brought it on.

"Shit, I was just doing my job," I said angrily, but I soon found out that even cops, who knew me, who I lived and worked with daily, were blaming me for not being more careful.

One of the project's head honchos finally got around to phoning me. "You going to charge him?" he asked in a clipped, bureaucratic voice.

I didn't know what to do. Nicky and I were tight. He hadn't lusted after me; it was a power thing, a control thing. And I was in the wrong place at the wrong time.

God, I wanted the asshole to pay. But a sexual assault conviction would only send him up for a few years. And if they charged

234

him, the investigation would be over. All that work and the possibility of him going to prison for life, down the drain.

Don't get mad—get even, I told myself.

"No, don't charge him," I responded coolly. "Let's really nail the bastard."

Maybe I was wrong. Maybe I should have stood up for myself then and there, Project Scorpion or no Project Scorpion. But my decision was to put the project first.

"Don't worry," Byron later assured me. "We'll remember you when we bust him."

Nicky and I saw each other a few days later. He gave me his big smile, and hugged me tightly like nothing had happened. I hugged him back. That was the way of the streets. In his twisted psyche, he figured he'd done nothing wrong. So I kept up the act. We were still friends. I was still a drug dealer, looking for another big score. And everything was okay.

A-Okay.

Time passed. Other dealers were set up. We charted the flow of drugs from the top on down, gathering information as we went.

Our lists were almost complete. It was getting to be time to make our busts. Meanwhile, Nicky started doing heroin. He'd used so much coke, he was practically brain dead. The heroin finished the job. Among the crazy stunts he did was shooting off his gun for no reason. One day, the cops found him running around the block where he lived—stark naked.

"I had to run out of my house because a man was inside trying to kill me," he told the arresting officers.

He was so stoned that he began hallucinating. When he sobered up, which wasn't often, and he was asked what he saw, he would laugh and blame the drug.

He was coming home late one night with a blonde on either arm when cops blocked the doorway to his house.

"What the hell you guys want?"

Nicky was surrounded. And the boys finally remembered me.

The prosecution offered twelve years without a trial.

"Take your offer and shove it," Nicky's lawyer said. "We can get him off."

The prosecutor stared at him but said nothing more.

I testified at Nicky's trial. The prosecutor tried to make it seem like I had turned crown agent and turned on Nicky for profit. It didn't work.

Because of what I'd done to put him there, Nicky wanted a piece of me so bad, he hired a private detective to help take me out. The man sat next to Nicky's lawyer in court every time I was on the stand, studying me. Not that Nicky worried about what I might say. As soon as his detective found me, I'd fall out a window.

Of course, it didn't happen that way. The police gave me their best security and lots of special treatment. Yes, it was in their best interests to do that, but I appreciated their efforts.

After it was all over, he was found guilty. His lawyer really ripped him off. Nicky owned whole city blocks, two or three homes and a few businesses. Only Nicky knows how much of it went to the lawyer's fees.

"Mr. Pugliese," said the judge, "I sentence you to life in prison." If he'd taken the deal, he would have been out long ago. Since Nicky's man had failed to get me, Nicky himself put out a contract on my life.

Project Scorpion eventually led to the destruction of drug rings in Canada, the United States and Europe. The very successful operation took a lot of drugs off the streets and put a lot of players in prison.

However, I felt mentally and physically tired. The delays, especially, had been very hard. The day of the sentencing, I was leaning on a column in the back of the courtroom when a young policewoman on court detail walked up to me.

"I'm Constable Danielle McLean. I wanted to tell you I think you're very brave and intelligent," she told me. "A lot of us around here think you could have been anything you wanted to be, and we'd like to know what your goal was as a child."

I paused, thinking of those long-ago days.

"There was a time when I wanted to be a doctor," I said.

"You would have made it, too, if you had had the education and the chance," Danielle said.

She looked admiringly at me and went on.

"But what you've become is even more important. You're a role model."

I stared at her, speechless, tears rising in my eyes.

A Short or Long Respite?

Mile zero of the Alaska Highway. Dawson Creek, British Columbia. I was there because I was bone tired. The pressures that had built up within me from doing undercover work had taken their toll. I'd come to Dawson Creek to lick my wounds, to rest, to regenerate, to think about retiring from undercover work for good.

For the first time since I could remember, doing nothing was enough. I lived with the Eskimos. I fished and slept and did little else until my savings ran out. Then I managed to find a job working as a program director for a native organization. The job required little effort and would suit me at least for a little while. Still, I spent most of my idle time thinking. One of my most recurrent thoughts was about getting officially pardoned for my past crimes.

After the Triad case, the idea of a pardon had been mentioned to me. At the time it didn't seem important, but now I realized it was—and is.

I have lived a productive life for over twenty years. I have taken risks in the drug wars that most others would not. I put my life on the line over and over again. I helped put a lot of bad guys away. I helped get millions of dollars worth of drugs off the streets, which in turn saved many people all over the world from falling into the abyss of drug abuse.

239

I have sacrificed my emotional and physical well-being in order to pay my debt to society. I feel I deserve a pardon. It would mean a lot to me. It would be the "thank you" I've never gotten.

Despite my need for peace and quiet, I still had to go to Ottawa several times to testify against some people who worked for Nicky. The long trips cost the government a small fortune. The airport runway—singular—in Dawson Creek was so short, jets couldn't land. I had to take small eight-seaters out. They shook all the way to Vancouver. By the time we landed, I was ready to kiss the ground.

Once in Vancouver, I changed to a real jet, which was destined for Toronto. From there, it was five hours motoring by car to Ottawa. I'd stay a few days and testify, then go back to exile in Dawson Creek.

The single engine plane from Vancouver to Dawson Creek mostly carried men: geologists, engineers and outfitters bringing supplies back to bush camps that were getting ready for the arrival of wealthy American hunters who wanted to bag some big game. The few women who traveled this route with them were largely government workers making their annual trip to the North Country beyond Dawson Creek, miners' wives going for a visit, and one or two women who lived in the North. The latter were usually going home after a trip to the city to see a medical specialist, shop or just visit family and friends.

As I traveled that route week after week, I noticed that coming out, everyone talked; but going back, everyone was very quiet. This happened, I realized, because we were going into another world, one that was silent, slow-moving; we had to mentally prepare for it. In the beginning, I liked that unwinding feeling, but after awhile it was starting to become deadening.

I finally decided to return to civilization, but not to work, settling in a town I knew well but in a different neighborhood where no one knew me. I continued to put psychical, if not physical, distance between the life of an undercover agent—which I had lived for so long—and the present. I wanted to think about my life—where I was going, where I had been.

I tried to assess the meaning of my work and the results, good and bad, of my career as an undercover: the bad guys I'd taken down; the tons of drugs I'd confiscated; the sad disappointment in my fellow human beings, especially those who were supposed to be on the right side of the law; the unexpected delight in my fellow human beings, especially those like the young police-woman at Nicky Pugliese's trial. The danger to my own life.

It didn't worry me that there were contracts out on my life, among them the Triad's, the Mafia's and Nicky Pugliese's. I knew no one was actively searching for me. If any hits were carried out, it would be only based on opportunity. That's how life-time contracts, the kind on my head, are handled.

The mobsters know that if they give the nod and I get whacked, there are plenty of law enforcement people who will know the culprits. The mobsters weigh the odds. And at times, they even cancel a hit if the odds aren't with them. Some, if given enough time, see reason. But I knew I could never depend on that. For the rest of my life, I could never let my guard down. It's second nature to me. I don't even find it a burden anymore.

It gives me some comfort to know that because of my efforts, Nicky is doing life in prison and has spent all his money on lawyers and paying for a few other hits on his peers. But I do take contracts seriously; we all know these guys can rise again.

However, my police sources tell me that Nicky is not making any friends in prison. The Jamaican posse has made an attempt against his life. There is always a power struggle for control in prison. So Nicky is being kept very busy trying to stay alive.

Do I have any fears? Of course. Fear is my friend. Only a fool is not afraid. The people I have gone after are career criminals. When you have been the cause of their undoing, as I have, you must accept the threat to your own life. It is a threat I live with today and always.

I know it all goes with the territory. The possibility of being imminently dead is a risk I accepted when I first got into the business of undercover work, and had previously lived with as a criminal. I was more prepared than are most undercover agents because I had walked this mine field all my life.

However, the question is where to go from here. Whether to go on, to continue striving for what's right and to accept the loneliness of a life in which you can never afford the luxury of friends or even a true soulmate, or to just quit.

I thought of the toll I had seen the work take on other officers and agents, including the leg work, the busts, the risk to life and limb. Hours, days and weeks when officers were away from their families, children growing up without parents; people living such a secret life that they only had each other to talk to, yet trying to stay out of each other's heads; surviving on three to five hours sleep a day and cheap takeout food; and the adrenal glands constantly working overtime.

At this point, I had only myself to care for, but if I wanted more someday—could I handle that *and* the work I had chosen? It would be almost impossible. And so, during the weeks that followed, my mind went back and forth, up and down. Still, I had come to no final conclusions about the future.

Then, one August day at summer's end, I had been out walking for hours, trying to rid myself of excess energy and to make some firm decisions. In my restless state, I had unknowingly covered mile after mile and now found myself in a neighborhood I knew well—the red light district.

Wearing only a thin, silver knit shirt and grey pants, I discovered to my surprise that the day was turning into night and I was shivering. Spotting Barnaby's Corner, a small, secluded bar where I had often met my contacts, I ducked in.

I sat down at the bar and ordered a brandy. As the hot, sweet liquid flowed down my throat and warmed me, I looked around. My eyes, as always, were fastened on the door.

As if by prearrangement, an old informant of mine, Alex Murray, and his girlfriend Cindy strode in. Alex, to put it succinctly, was a pimp and Cindy, a well-endowed bottle blond, was his main woman. Though they sat next to me, they did not notice me, because of the dim lighting and the conversation they were so engrossed in.

"Dammit, you ought to stay off the streets for awhile," Alex was saying.

"Yeah, and how am I supposed to make a living for you and—"

"For *us*," Alex interrupted.

Nice touch, I thought.

"Well, it was your roommate Kira last week. Next time it might be you. He's a serial killer, you know, as well as a rapist."

"I told her not to go out that night."

Alex looked up, "Did you tell the police any of that?"

"Are you crazy? They don't even know for sure who she is. You think I want them to contact us? You? She was one of *your* girls, remember."

"I remember," he said uncomfortably. "I hate thinking of Kira dead, and that last guy she was with—some accountant! I knew something was wrong with him; he looked like a wimp with those watery green eyes and those hands he kept licking with his tongue every minute . . . ."

There was something about this description that jarred me. The man Alex described seemed so familiar. I leaned toward Alex and tapped him on the shoulder. He turned.

"Dorothy!" he said, surprised.

"How are you? Haven't seen you for a long while."

"I'm fine, and I've been away. Listen, I hate to bother you, but that guy you were talking about . . . I think he reminds me of someone."

"Yeah?"

"Yeah. You wouldn't know his name, would you, Cindy?"

She shrugged. "Are you kidding? When do the johns ever give us their real names?"

I laughed. I had a pretty good idea who this john was though—and where he could be found.

At home, later that night, I didn't hesitate. I immediately called the Contained Intelligence Unit.

A few days later, I entered the multi-storied high-rise downtown where ACP Accounting, a firm specializing in estate planning, had their headquarters.

"Yes, can I have your name, please?" asked the pretty blond receptionist, looking up.

I knew the person she saw exactly fit the part of a well-off, slightly overweight woman with reddish-blond hair in her forties, wearing too much jewelry. She wouldn't recognize that my cheekbones are high, showing a bit of my Mic Mac Indian background, or that my hair is dyed and the natural black at the roots displays a little of my African heritage. Still, with my creamy skin, I could be anything—Scottish like my grandparents, Greek, Italian; just about any nationality or ethnic group you could think of.

I smiled shyly at her. "Sally," I said with a slight stammer. "Sally Ann Taggart."

"Oh yes, you have a lunch appointment with Clark Barnett."

I nodded. "Unfortunately, I have a serious illness," I confided, "and I'm supposed to discuss planning my estate for my children."

"You'll just *love* Clark," she said, trying too hard to be enthusiastic. "He's so . . . ," she searched for the right word, "empathetic."

"So I've heard," I murmured, and took a seat.

Not long afterwards, a small man in his late thirties, whose body had already turned soft and lumpy, emerged from an inner office.

"Ah, Mrs. Taggart. I am so glad I shall have the chance to help you plan for the future." He put out his hand to shake mine. His was limp and wet as I took it, just as I knew it would be. I had a gut feeling this was the serial killer.

"Shall we go?"

244

"I'm ready," I answered with a slight smile. "I hope you are, too."

As he helped me rise, I looked into his vapid, watery green eyes . . . and all thoughts of retirement faded from my mind.